Vanessa,

Thank you for your interest in my book.

I hope you enjoy it!

Adrianne M. Murchison

Author Adrianne Murchison's personal desire for a deeper understanding of the complex relationships between black men and women, as well as their impact on the children of those unions, was the impetus for this book. Ultimately interviewing more than 50 people, Murchison asked participants in her informal study about their perceptions of personal responsibility, family life, and intimate relationships, with an eye toward contributing to a healing process that might address the issues and obstacles facing black couples and black youth today.

Although Murchison has worked in the investment industry for 13 years, her true interests lie in community issues. She has volunteered her time and energy to many projects, including the Park Avenue Women's Shelter in New York, the East Harlem Tutorial Program, Covenant House, and the Innocence Project.

A Buffalo, New York native, Murchison attended college in Atlanta and has resided in New York City for 10 years.

TABLE OF CONTENTS

KALIEDING

ON THE ROAD TO

HAPPINESS

Copyright © 1997 Adrianne Marie Murchison

KALIEDING

ON THE ROAD TO

HAPPINESS

Kaleidoscope—1. a tubular optical instrument in which loose bits of colored glass at the end of the tube are reflected in mirrors so as to display ever-changing symmetrical patterns as the tube is rotated.
2. *a continually shifting pattern, scene or the like*

Collide—1. to strike one another, or one against the other with a forceful impact; crash. 2. to clash; conflict

*To the Lord God, Jesus Christ. Through you
I found the insight and the words.*

Acknowledgements

This book was written and published with the support and guidance of many who believe in me. My financial contributors did not hesitate when called upon and often exceeded my expectations.

Thank you G., Michelle, Tonya and Sam, Russ, Barry H., Sallie, Monica and Chris, Mr. R., Christopher, Rod Hunter, Miesha Mays, Ayesha Strickland, Mark Mason, Troy Datcher, Sidney Lake, Cathy Green, Tracy Chamblee, Sam Zimmerman, Kelly Chase, Daniel Dickin, Pat Long, Yvonne Anderson and Mary Alice.

Thank you Patti and Bruce for loving me. You are my biggest fans.

Thank you Leo, Donna Quadri, Elise Donner-Smith and Melvin Williams whose support, advice and referrals helped to make this book a reality.

Thank you Pat Felitti and the Morton's of Chicago Management and staff for your kindness, support and encouragement: Constance Kazee, Paul Whiteley, Lynn Kennedy, Abigail Kaufman, A.J. Tissian, Jerry Garcia, Stephen Borden, Bob Mundy, Christine Achillo, Donald Lafferty, Carie Scott, Shelford Mitchell and many others whose interest and positive words strengthened me along the way.

Thank you to my Bear Stearns friends including, Gloria Archibald, Joann Howfield, Kathy Scarabaggio, Stephanie Halvax, Laura Solimene, Jerry Deignan, Ed Lauffer, Ardavan Mobasheri, Julie Patterson, Roseanna De Fazio and countless others.

Amy Garvey, my editor and Rick Banks, my photographer and friend: your professionalism and flexibility gave me peace of mind in knowing this work would turn into everything I hoped for.

Thank you to everyone I interviewed. Your honesty and candor provided a level of understanding that not only enabled me to present this topic in a different light, it also taught me the importance of examining my own strengths and weaknesses.

i

Thank you Mom (I love you so much), Dad, Russ, Jeff, Laurie and the rest of my family and close friends including beloved Montine and Ladie Whitaker, you strengthen me and help me to continue to reach for higher highs.

And finally, Tonya Guzman, you are an inspiration and a reminder that God's love will provide.

Special Thanks to:

Charlie Rose

The Honorable Minister Louis Farrakhan

Preface

"If you don't give somebody the benefit of the doubt and take it to the end of the road, you'll never know... " Charlie Rose

I will always remember a scene from the play *Fires in the Mirror*. In that scene, Anne Deavere Smith portrayed a juror in the Rodney King civil trial discussing the hostility and animosity felt throughout the diverse twelve-member group. She explained that after the jurors vented their pent-up emotions and preconceived ideas about each other, amazingly they were able to put their differences aside and sit down to deliberate. At the time I couldn't relate to the experience of successfully airing out differences and then moving forward. However, since then, in small instances, I have discovered that indeed can happen.

That is the hope behind this effort. That black men and women can hear each other and still care enough to learn from what they hear and move towards one another, rather than further apart.

Love is the nature of our being. It's our center, our core. Some people allow it to flow naturally, others suppress their instincts to give and receive it. But when confronted by its power, in its purest, most genuine form, it's impossible to be unaffected.

Men and women may have different mindsets when they come together. She may wonder, "Is he the one?" And physical attraction may be more important than a relationship in his mind. But the power of love, vulnerability, and the desire to be cherished are not far away. Otherwise we'd play fewer games, put up less walls, and let down our defenses.

This book is simply a statement of how the men and women interviewed perceive their intimate and professional relationships. It is a step towards giving each other a chance when we come together, and overcoming fears and differences in order to give ourselves a fighting chance at happiness. It's about enlightenment, acceptance, and respect.

Everyone seems to agree there are problems between African-American men and women. Some would say we are in a crisis situation. I hold an idealistic belief that men and women can accept each other, love each other, and come together once again to produce healthy families within viable communities.

One day during a lengthy discussion my physician commented that in her view men and women don't recognize when and why they are incompatible. She said a young professional woman who was raised by educated parents in a middle-class home will naturally encounter differences with her male peer who grew up in the projects in the midst of crime and violence, and who represents the first generation in his family to receive a college education and embark on a successful career. Her point: their life experiences are vastly different and will affect the way they approach and deal with intimate relationships.

This made sense to me, but it was also disturbing. The implication was it would be pointless for this couple to pursue their attraction. Their different life experiences would doom their fate. But we all have different experiences. Even people of similar backgrounds can experience them differently. The key is we have to give ourselves an opportunity to explore our differences truthfully, to discover if there is a commonality, a lasting attraction, a foundation to build upon. Otherwise we deny ourselves the benefit of the doubt, which can be fulfillment and growth.

The question remains, how do we go about resolving the problems? How do we stop the madness? Our ability to resolve the issues is as important as the issues themselves. There is enough blame to go around, and around, and around. In order to achieve effective resolutions we must first consider our personal role in the current state of affairs. This is crucial to a successful healing process.

Over fifty men and women of color from diverse backgrounds and varying ages were asked how they felt about their struggles, their place in life, children, relationships, and the state of the black community. To my surprise, men expressed a wider range of emotions than expected on their involvement with black women, including love, anger, rawness, pain and understanding. The love that many women revealed for black men was sandwiched between their frustration and anger. As a black woman, I naturally bring biases to the table. My voice is meant to reflect the hurt and disappointment that lies beneath much of what was expressed by women. Nevertheless, the objective is to stay on the path of truth, which is always lying there when a person is ready to take it.

Both groups seemed to find the interview experience cathartic; however, most had a much better perception of their counterpart's shortcomings than their own.

Many women believe they are the hard workers. They are always trying to do the right thing in their relationships while coming up with the short end of the stick, most of the time. They don't think they should have to put forth any further effort to make a relationship work. Black women want to see black men approach them in a manner that demonstrates respect and appreciation, because experience has shown them there are endless trials they must endure, unnecessarily. As a result, a woman's focus may never shift from her frustrations to what she may have done to hurt the relationship.

On the other hand, it matters to black men how black women feel about themselves, black men, and the relationship. They are aware of how they may have hurt their relationships, but they would prefer not to go there. A man might say, "What's the point? What's done is done. I apologized. I love her, she's a beautiful black woman and I respect her." That's wonderful, but unless they are willing to step on those hot coals and deal with what actually transpired in their situation, it would be like placing band-aids on gunshot wounds.

Acknowledging that there are problems between African-American men and women which need to be addressed inevitably means critical perceptions and opinions will be a part of the process. Thankfully, in keeping with the ultimate objective of healing the wounds, most comments were direct and honest. In addition, however, they were also often disturbing and provocative.

Men and women of color are capable of overcoming their initial objections to contrary opinions. And they will be able to consider and take stock in what is said. Other interested parties, such as white men and women, may not wish to go beneath the surface of racial comments to see the reality of what has manifested between black men and women out of feelings of powerlessness, rejection, hurt, disrespect, and much more. I raise this concern because in spite of our prejudices across the cultures, friendships, and relationships are formed with the very people we complain about. I think it attests to our nature as caring human beings.

How black men and women feel about white men and women with respect to interracial relationships is a secondary or side issue to how they internalize their perception of the loss of an important component of their culture whom they love, the black man and the black woman.

People often seem curious to know if my personal life inspired me to write this book. My concern for the survival of the black family and the men in my past and present have served as catalysts for this undertaking. Hey, I expected to be married with children years ago. And although I'm still young, time is passing and I find myself asking God, "When?"

Marriage and family have always been what I wanted most for myself. But that equation must include love. As long as I can remember I've been searching for my "Prince Charming." Maybe I should have outgrown this notion, but my parents taught me that family was one of life's greatest treasures. Years ago, when my father passed away, I reflected on my many childhood memories and since then I've had an increased desire to recreate the family security I felt within my home.

I grew up believing women were entitled to everything men were entitled to. My thoughts and feelings were as legitimate as any man's opinion. This was not because my parents had equality in their marriage, but because in my eyes they raised me as an equal to my older brothers, although my brothers saw it as favoritism towards me. My parents also taught me through examples they set in their professional lives that I must stand up for myself and my rights. I've brought this mindset to the table in dealing with many of the men in my life. Being involved with men who may agree with it in theory, but not in practice, has been frustrating. Many of my experiences have been with men who seemed more comfortable if they could perceive me as less intelligent than themselves. My nature is to react with, "No, that's not right!" Which, I've learned, can make matters worse because of how many men were raised.

Believing I have a lot to offer a mate based on what I possess inside, I was baffled as to why I was not successful in finding Mr. Right. The scenario usually went something like this: I'd meet someone who I'd become excited about. We'd get along great at first. And then suddenly things would go awry. Why? A misconception held by one or the both of us.

At the start of this project I had already concluded the problems lay within men. And to be honest, I set out to discover their problem. In fairness I wanted to get both perspectives: women's frustrations and men's explanations. Instead I found myself on a journey that has led to insight, discovery, and hard-learned lessons. Most pleasantly surprising was discovering the love and allegiance black men feel towards black women, regardless of where interactions have taken their relationships.

A self-supporting man and woman desire the same things from each other. Love, affection, respect, consideration and adoration balanced with reality, acceptance, and timely acquiescence. They fight almost identical battles in society, although to different degrees, and yet knowing and sharing these struggles some find it impossible to just let go and open up, giving what they desperately want to receive themselves.

One would think this bond would create a level of comfort and trust rather than the deep divide that exists among men and women as a group and within relationships. But listening to men discuss their perspectives has of course given me a different sensitivity to them than I previously had. This sensitivity has created a deeper awareness, but it has not, as I am often asked, provided me with solutions to all the problems that plague my relationships, or anyone else's. It is my belief that God's ultimate will is unknown and therefore no one can possibly possess all of the answers. My experience has been that attempting to assume what He has planned can in fact delay His plan.

In the past I tried to assume by saying, "Just give me a sign!" Then I incorrectly thought my relationships were meant to work out when I received the sign I asked for. Although, I must admit, He probably did answer me once by saying "No," in His way, but I didn't want to hear it.

I had gone to Saint Patrick's Cathedral one day during my lunch hour. While there I asked God to tell me what to do about my relationship with Sonny. "Let me know one way or another," I asked, "if we are meant to be... if I should stick it out." As I walked back to my office, I bumped into Sonny. Our offices were in close proximity, but we rarely ran into each other on the street. When talking, he invited me to dinner that night. Of course I thought this was a part of my sign.

At dinner he told me that he cared for me, but... he didn't want the committed relationship I wanted. Well, there was my answer. I appreciated his candor, but inside I would not accept that as my "no" from above. If I had accepted it and left it at that, I would have saved myself a few years of heartache.

In a separate relationship, I incorrectly assumed things were meant to work out with Kenny when I prayed for a call from him at a specific time on a specific day, a time when ordinarily he would not call. When that prayer was answered, I knew I was meant to be patient and hang in there. But I was wrong again. A few months later I moved on. Shortly afterwards I discovered the scripture, "True Wisdom," which has taught me not to question God, no matter how difficult my faith or circumstances may be. I must trust God.

True Wisdom
Jeremiah, 17: 5-10

Thus says the Lord:

Cursed is the man who trusts in human beings,

who seeks his strength in flesh,

whose heart turns away from the Lord.

He is like the barren bush in the desert, that enjoys no change of season,

But stands in a lava waste, a salt and empty earth.

Blessed is the man who trusts in the Lord, whose hope is the Lord.

He is like a tree planted beside the waters that stretches out its roots to the stream:

It fears not the heat when it comes, its leaves stay green;

In the year of the drought it shows no distress, but still bears fruit.

More tortuous than all else is the human heart,

beyond remedy; who can understand it?

I, the Lord alone probe the mind and test the heart,

to reward everyone according to his ways, according to the merit of his deeds...

So, in my humble opinion, a person's most promising hope for a successful relationship is to be reasonably equipped with the tools to build a healthy foundation and partnership with their mate. I use the word "hope" because relationships are complex. I'd like to believe that I have the traits of one side of a fruitful relationship, but frankly I still get confused. For example, it has taken me years to understand that it takes two people to make a relationship a success. You may possess all of the gifts to give your relationship a healthy chance, but if the other person is not in it with you, there's nothing to build on. All efforts are fruitless.

This may seem like common sense. But it is a lesson I learned literally through trial and error. I made a habit of becoming involved with "the one." Kind of a prototype of the same person over and over again. I'd fall in love while sensing his fear and resistance, and then try in vain to convince him to commit to me, marry me, love me. In the end, through the grace of God and despite the hurt, I realized I didn't really want him. He couldn't make me happy and I walked away with dignity and peace. I repeated the cycle for several years until I became so drained and intolerant, I began to cut men off at the first scent of fear and resistance in them.

And then I met Josh.

I was ripe for a fulfilling relationship. I had been praying, "Just give me something to work with... please!" But that was the beginning of the most difficult year of Josh's life. The woman he'd been involved with for seven years left him (in his mind, unexpectedly). His brother, whom he loved but had been estranged from for seven years, died after a long illness. (Fortunately they had a brief heartfelt reunion.) The rest of his family was pushing his buttons and he was enduring upheavals at his job.

We met shortly after his break-up and before he reconciled with his brother. The red flag was waving prominently, I'm sure. But Josh was vulnerable, open, and leaning on me. He sensed my fear and pain from previous relationships and he encouraged me to lean on him, too. Despite the crises and the fears we became soulmates and he was everything of substance I wanted.

And then he shut down. He became closed and kept me at a distance. It was like an elevator at the 50th floor that suddenly drops to the 25th and then *gradually* descends to the basement. It's on automatic and you can hit the buttons as much as you like, but it's going *down*.

I loved him and I found it impossible to turn away because I felt in my bones that he loved me, too. Months passed and I was still there trying to let him know I believed in him. Our love for each other, and the fact that all of my attempts to make the relationship work proved irrelevant since there was no effort put forth on his part. When it ended, I told him I was "hurting over a relationship that really wasn't."

When I think of a one-sided effort, a friend's comments come to mind. He said, "You want a strong supportive partner by your side at the altar. Not someone hobbling up and resisting as you pull them along."

Have you ever known anyone who was terribly ill and inevitably going to pass away? You have all the information. You're allowed time to prepare, but when they go, not only are you filled with sorrow and a longing for their presence, but with anger and confusion wondering, *"Why!?"* You did all the research. You have all of the facts. But you don't have a complete understanding of why they are gone.

This book is a looking glass into reasons behind certain behavior. The title reflects the *kaleidoscope* of perspectives from the people interviewed, and the frustrations that can be felt when two people emotionally, mentally, and even physically *collide* on the road to love and fulfillment. View it as a testament to how men and women feel about each other and more importantly how they feel about themselves, which is an integral part of any relationship. From that point you may open your mind and discover a new sensitivity, awareness, and eventually... your answers.

1

When the Wind Blows

"… like the man who built his house on the ground without any foundation. When the torrent rushed upon it, it immediately fell and was completely destroyed."

The Gospel According to Luke

Non-minorities, people who are not of color, are sometimes a little bit cynical when they learn of the topic of this book. Many have said that most couples share common problems that are not exclusive to any particular race. So why target African-Americans as if they have issues that are specific to them?

Unfortunately, African-Americans do have issues that are specific to them. Young white boys and girls can dare to dream of their future college experiences, or life as family men and women, or careers as teachers, policemen, doctors, attorneys, or even president. Many young black boys and girls cannot dare to dream of these lifestyles. Today their reality is surviving another day in their neighborhood and their fantasy is of a life as a basketball star or music artist. And if you travel along the spectrum toward the children who are the product of stable homes and will have opportunities for a successful future, you will pass others who have enormous potential but are trapped in their environment. Still others struggle to climb out as they carry hurt, anger, and resentment for their parents who they feel created this madness.

I see these children and I say to myself, "These are children of my generation." And I can't help but wonder what happened. I was allowed to dream and aspire, as were my brothers. There were gangs and violence when I was coming up, but I don't recall the self-hatred.

Once, while volunteering, I listened to a group of young men speak to teens about their efforts to overcome their crimes and violent pasts. Seated in a circle, each told his story and had long ago accepted accountability for his actions. Everyone brought up the absence of love in their lives as they grew up. To my surprise they did not discuss the lack of role models, money, and educational or job opportunities when describing their households. They only mentioned love. Each believed it was the absence of love that set him on the path of self-destruction.

The young man sitting beside me began to tell his story. He had killed someone. Pointlessly. His mother's boyfriend gave him his first gun on his 13th birthday so he could feel like a man.

It seemed to me fear should have been my natural reaction. I was sitting next to this person who had taken a life. What I felt was sadness, and a connection as I do when any young life is taken away violently. It is all senseless. Every aspect of black on black crime is personally internalized on some level in the black community. Especially when it is black youth on black youth. The mourning does not stop with the lost life of the victim. There is a mix of emotions directed at the wasted life of the perpetrator. He or she came into this world as innocent as the next child. But something went terribly wrong.

Still, there is polarization and confusion among those who are succeeding in society regarding those who may be trapped in a cycle of destruction. The feedback I received from many men and women I interviewed was of deep concern for the unfortunate realities children are facing and a fear they will be written off as the "lost generation." But some are unclear and untrusting of the truth of these realities as portrayed in the media. And others are of the opinion that kids today are no worse off than kids were twenty years ago; they may have more of an advantage. Peter, 37, of Atlanta, feels positive kids are grasping more and they are more goal-oriented and independent; "Our generation had help from our parents who made a way for us."

Leo, 44 and a stockbroker in New York, said his concerns run differently. "I find myself hoping that life for them holds everything they want. Because at my age, having dealt out here as a black man and realizing the problems that exist for me, I'm hoping things are going to be different for them. Because I see the inequities in life. There are too many people who can live their lives without the concerns that I concern myself with. Having the freedom to say 'no,' or being able to say, 'f— you,' or being able to do what you want to do and be judged solely upon your merit as an individual, not by your color or your sexual preference, et cetera... I just think it's absolutely tremendous."

Becoming involved with a troubled youth set on a path of destruction requires an emotional investment that Leo is aware can become overwhelming. He offered to help Kyle, a youth from my teen group, obtain a low-level position with his company. He thought this would open up an entirely new world for Kyle by simply getting him out of his neighborhood every day and into a professional environment.

4

In spite of Kyle's initial eagerness, he did not show up for his interview with personnel. He hadn't even gone home the night before. Although Leo had put himself out to set things up, after a three-way conversation with Kyle and his mentor Mark, Leo rescheduled the interview for the following day.

Kyle kept the appointment and afterwards he told Leo he thought everything had gone well. Later that afternoon Leo telephoned me and said he needed to see me immediately. Distraught would be an understatement to describe Leo's state of mind. Personnel had called to let him know they did not think Kyle had completed his high school equivalency test as he told us he had, and more importantly they didn't think he knew how to read or write. "A young black male trying to make it out here and he can't read or write!? He's just trying to get over!? Playing a con game?" Leo said in bewilderment. He wanted me to answer him but I didn't know what to say. I understood what he was asking. But he was feeling something I couldn't completely understand. He had a glimpse of the reality of many black males and he was not only pained by it, he felt a coming extinction of black men in society.

As time went on Leo spoke of Kyle as a con artist, a joke, and a danger when I told him Kyle was working with small children at the volunteer center. Mark and the center administrators believe Kyle is literate but set himself up to fail out of fear of the unknown. Several months down the road, he suddenly stopped working and he was eventually incarcerated.

Many people say focus on the very young. Catch them before they're corrupted and lose their innocence.

At what point do you give up on people, on children, youths? Babies and small children are so innocent, we feel and care about them so deeply. At what point do we stop caring and cast them off as the lost generation? At what age? Is it when they lose their innocence? If that's lost at 14, is a life over? Do we stop trying to help them and nurture them? Or is it 16 or 18? Can we afford to do that?

I had an opportunity to sit down with a group of young men in a young fathers program in the Bronx. They range in age from 17 to 23 years old and describe themselves as kids who grew up in the streets hanging with the wrong crowd. All come from single-parent homes headed by their mothers, except one who says, "I grew up with both my parents... My Pops use to beat my Mom... He was president of one the worst gangs in the Bronx. I grew up the hard way. I was raised in the streets... and that's not fun."

It was enlightening to sit down with kids who are supposed to be from the "lost generation" and discuss how they feel about themselves. They have a lot of self-worth and it was disheartening to hear them tell of teachers and policemen who said they'd never amount to anything. They couldn't help but internalize it. Each one told me of incidents when a cop held a gun to his head and told him he was nothing but a "nigger" or a "spic". Johnny said a policeman had him pinned down with the gun in his face, saying, "I hate you fucking spics, man... I should just kill you right now. It would be one less spic I have to deal with."

And now, as they distance themselves from the streets, they are working very hard to have an active role in their children's lives. They want to be fathers to their children because their fathers were not there for them. Alan said, " I tried to talk to my Mom when I started having sex and she was just not the right person... I want my son to come to me when he has something to talk about." And yet the peer pressure is strong. These young men are looked upon as weak if they try to support their children. "It takes guts... It takes heart. It takes a lot of courage to come through the block with your son, because a lot of people out there don't take care of their kids," says Billy, who has come to the realization that love is more important than money. "I want to be able to give my son love... because money don't mean everything."

The problems the "lost generation" is facing are a direct result of the generation that precedes them. They have learned through observation not to place great value or trust in partnerships or commitment to the opposite sex. They are also learning self-preservation as they watch us distance ourselves from their plight.

The African-American community is complex. The struggles are numerous. There is no single answer. I do know the family unit begins with the union of two individuals; for our purposes here, a man and a woman. It does not begin with the mother and the child or the father and the child. The man and the woman must come together before the children can be created. If two people can't come together and lay a healthy foundation, that union cannot sustain itself when conflicts arise.

2

TRADITION!
TRADITION?

"The Black Woman" by Louis Farrakhan (excerpt from Essence, January 1972)

... We cannot understand the role of man and woman until we go to the essence of man and woman, which is their very nature. By nature the man is created to work for the woman, to provide for her; and by nature the woman is created to console the man, to bring him quiet of mind.

When a woman truly loves a man, she loves that man because he is able to secure her, provide for her, and to maintain her in every way. In this state of security, she is a peace; and this by nature makes her desire to serve that man who has secured her, by consoling him, cooking for him, keeping his home, taking care of him and rearing his children. The woman in this natural state of security does not look upon her natural duty toward the man as slavery; nor does she look upon this duty as demeaning.

A natural woman accepts this duty as an honor, as a way to do for the man who is doing for her and has made her secure. Man and woman functioning properly in their natural roles are at peace with each other and go forward as one...

... The black woman does not need to be liberated from the rule of the black man, for she controls him, she regards him almost as a child. But the black man does need to be liberated from the rule of his open enemy and oppressor.

... It is not that the black woman desires to rule the black man; she steps in to do what the black man has been unable to do. The black woman actually wants to see the black man take his place.

... The black woman today wants a man who can secure her in every respect. She wants a man who is morally strong, a man who can teach her and guide her, a man who will rule with her in wisdom and justice. She wants a man who will love her, be kind to her and patient with her.

When I came across this excerpt of an article written years ago, I thought it would be interesting if it was read during the interviews for this book to see how it was interpreted. To avoid bias the author's name was withheld until after the piece was read.

With a few exceptions, most women strongly disagreed with the article and most men approved of it. Linda's comments — "Does this come with barf bags? I can barely finish it!" — were typical of those who interpreted the article as dictating roles, the woman's as the housewife who cooks and cleans, and the man's as the ruling breadwinner. They viewed it as unrealistic, outdated, and often asked if it was written by "that woman" who condoned men slapping women around from time to time.

"This is the '90s," many said. Not only are women on equal ground with men, but men find the qualities that put them there more appealing than those reflected in the article.

Diana, a woman who fits the mold of today's modern black woman, was not insulted. She said, "We are such a literal people. If one is okay with the essence, one could evolve to a deeper essence of what takes place."

The essence of what takes place. When I first read the excerpt I thought it captured exactly what takes place between black men and women. My interpretation may not be what the author was trying to convey, however to me it says that a woman wants to feel at peace in her world. She is at peace when she has love and security. Love and security can entail many things. In this case, if a woman feels that she and her man truly love each other and he is fulfilling all of her needs, most importantly her emotional needs, then she is at peace. If she is happy in her relationship with him and she truly loves him, then she wants to make him happy as well. She wants to do for him. This does not necessarily mean cooking and cleaning. But it could mean anything from surprising him with an erotic evening to just "consoling" him.

Often women insist on being looked upon as equal to men. We're equal in the sense that our strengths offset the others' weaknesses. But we are not the same. Since women are not as physically strong as men, and different expectations are placed upon them, they exercise their intuition and emotional strength much more often than men. Therefore a woman may be able to control a man or a situation. Whereas men, on the other hand, are physically stronger and the expectations placed upon them do not demand that they exercise these senses as often as women.

The expectation of man is to be the protector and the provider. In the real world, the black man may not be able to do this. Often you find, "... it is not that the black woman desires to rule the black man; she steps in to do what the black man has been unable to do." As a result, he often becomes frustrated and finds that he needs to be "liberated" from the black woman as well as the person he perceives to be "his open enemy and oppressor."

More than ever I agree with the last paragraph. If a woman wants a man, she wants someone who shares her values. It says, "A man who can teach her and guide her, a man who will rule with her in wisdom and justice." Well, if they are together in exercising wisdom and justice, then she is a teaching and guiding force in the family also. Lastly, "She wants a man who will love her, be kind to her and patient with her." We all want this from our loved ones.

This is not the 1970s, when the excerpt was written, but the black family structure has not reshaped itself to the extent that we have completely disconnected from the values with which many of us were raised. Values that gave us our culture, the Spirit of God, and direction, often within a family that was, if nothing else, dysfunctional. As we examine ourselves when we consider our problems with one another, we must also reflect on our upbringing, including the values that were instilled in us and how they impact our relationships.

Sam, who has been married over 40 years commented on a surprising consistency that ran through my interviewing process and possibly the root of the problem among couples today. In general, men were eager to discuss the problems that plague black men and women. While many have specific gripes, the overwhelming issue was their desire to have a sense that they are needed, that they have control over their households and their lives, and most of all their need to feel believed in by their mates. Conflict seems to arise when they are doubted and questioned. Then their sense of control is lost.

Women's views were unexpectedly varied. Those who were concerned had a wider scope of issues with black men than men had with women. But some were hesitant to discuss the subject. And others who were married or in committed relationships were indifferent because they did not see themselves as being directly affected.

These contrasts mirror Sam's perspective that each generation has raised their sons or placed burdens upon them to become the providers or heads of their households. This has been in direct conflict with the changing role of women in society over the past 30 to 40 years. And he said, frankly, he wouldn't want to walk in my shoes today as a black woman hoping to settle down with a black man because, "The man doesn't know what to look for and it's very confusing having different women with different points of view and expectations." Men, being ego-driven, are threatened by this changing role of women. "Educated men feel life is hard enough, they may as well go for the money because there are enough women out there looking for sex to satisfy their needs."

Sam saw the black family begin to break up with his generation, after the Civil Rights Movement, as the community moved away from the church and turned to the government to fulfill its needs. Women were continuing their education in large numbers; " You couldn't tell a woman who has just completed her education to choose homemaking and childrearing as a vocation." This was Sam's dilemma with his wife. "I was raised where everything was geared towards making me the head of the household. Master of the house. You can imagine when this person with a college education starts telling me what she wants to do... There was no way I could comprehend she wasn't going to take care of the kids and I wasn't going to bring home the bacon."

Sam's wife had a career, but she stayed home with the children during their formative years. Sam had a difficult time adjusting to her goals. He was raised in the church and as far as he was concerned, his wife's goals were not a part of the sacrament of marriage. "... Not knowing how to talk about it, or even how to put my finger on it to say, 'Look woman, you either do this or I'm going to knock you upside your head.'... There was no way I could reconcile my morals with her expectations. " He said they learned to make accommodations. And it was that factor more than communication that has helped their marriage to endure over the past 40 years.

Dr. Henry McCurtis, Director of Education in the Department of Psychiatry at Harlem Hospital in New York, cannot agree with this concept. He is uncomfortable with the tendency to minimize the prevailing problems within the African-American community and oversimplify the solutions. "That argument is a popular formulation to explain a lot of things," he said. "It is a fact there have been tremendous changes in the social roles and status. I'm sure it has had profound repercussions in all aspects of our lives, love, work, etc... But to say that something as pervasive as that is the cause... I would be afraid that it would present something so vastly complex as this thing that you're talking about in terms of the change in the dynamics between men and women... that we might be led into thinking that we understand all that it is about."

Dr. McCurtis continued, "What do men and women born after 1946 know about women's changing roles? Everything that they've seen has been the norm... Frederick Douglass saw different roles... People in World

War I saw different roles. But post World War I, we've seen women doing damn near everything that anybody else can do. And it has been progressive certainly since the '60s. So what is this business about our becoming distant and disoriented because women are suddenly changing their roles? We haven't seen anything new. How are [men] confused?"

We are a long way from the 1940s and the 1960s. There are a larger number of college-educated black men to complement educated black women, if they so choose. And one would hope this would mean that men have evolved in their perspective of women. Still, Sam's mind-set was echoed among the men I interviewed. In fact, like many other parents of his generation, he raised his son, who is now in his 30s, to be the head of the household. The provider. In that role it wouldn't be unnatural for the man to look upon his mate as an unequal partner or unlikely that the two would come to the table with different expectations.

Greg, 35, a freelance fashion photographer in Atlanta who won't marry until he feels financially secure, agrees with Sam's view that men carry the burden of the "breadwinner" in the household. "This may be from the old school, but I would like to take care of my family solely, if necessary. I'd naturally like a woman to... bring something to the table with me. But I want to be able to take care of my family."

During our interview, Greg raised interesting points about how essential it is to be open-minded in relationships, especially as two people are getting to know each other. As we talked, I imagined his open-mindedness was tested on a regular basis. His ideal woman is someone who is confident, intelligent, versatile, and above all down-to-earth. I wondered how this modern woman will contrast or complement Greg's traditional view as the "final decision-maker."

After reading the Farrakhan article he said, "I don't look at the ideal situation as the man ruling the woman, or one ruling the other. You've got a man who is the head of his household. But all decisions that are made are discussed between the two. Ultimately he's going to have the final say on it. But it's not like it should be a dictatorship... There definitely should be a team. You and I. It's not, 'You are my subordinate and you do what I say.' That just breeds contempt."

16

Rene, 30, an attorney in New York, says men, "... need to challenge themselves. The 'I was raised to believe' thing only goes so far... I can't tell you how many times I've had some conflict with a brother and he'll tell me, ' Well, my grandmother told me...' We have to determine whether or not that's viable. And if you find that is getting in the way of something that is vital and important in your life, like your relationship with another person, then it seems to me that is definitely cause to reconsider what you have been taught.

"Because maybe that worked in the '50s, '60s, '70s and with some people today, but the reality is we live in a country where unless a man is making a lot of money, it's difficult for a family to live on the salary of one person... You've got to be willing to deal with each other as equals. There's no way I'm going home earning what I'm earning and clocking 80 hours a week, so I can have some man tell me what to do, just because his mama told him that's the way things are supposed to be. Re-examine that."

We are products of our environment. Many women were raised to be independent in households where our fathers were the image of the provider and the protector, and our mothers appeared to continuously sacrifice and nurture the family. Given a free rein of independence and growth black women have not emerged as tolerant and passive as their mothers were. Many have a reasonable semblance of financial freedom and, like Rene, do not need a man to support them financially.

That does not mean women don't want a perception of their man as the provider and the cornerstone of their financial structure. More and more self-sufficient women are choosing not to return to full-time work, if they return at all, following the birth of their children. And the reasons are not solely to spend quality time with the family. They have decided they don't want the stress, or they want less of it, and they have a choice now because their husbands are accepting and carrying the financial weight of the family.

And so as Sam suggests, a man may be beset with a host of expectations from a black woman. He's not providing for the same type of woman his father may have provided for. To begin with, their economic base is probably larger. He's with a woman whose judgment, control, and power were respected at the workplace; a woman who is not tolerant of inequality, and yet wants to be taken care of. When it's all said and done, she's striving for the best of everything.

Rene admits she's conflicted because she enjoys her independence and yet she wants to enjoy all of the fruits of a having a family, which she knows will be her priority.

Leo, a father of four, said the lack of employment opportunities for his wife required him to be the sole income provider in their household during a two-year period when their family was smaller. He likens the black woman's dilemma to a candy store of 1,001 choices. They walk in and they see all the choices of candy and, "... they don't know what the f— they want. 'I want love, I want money, I want recognition, I want power, I want children.' " In frustration he adds, "You know what they end up doing? Becoming hogs! They want all the f——g candy. It's not enough to eat a little here and a little there. They want it all... " And most importantly they want their man to provide it for them. Leo thinks they want the man to say, " 'Go in there, honey, and whatever you want, you take.' " He continued, "and there can be the Emotional Section, the Physical Section, the Mental Section, the Financial Section. Well again, you know what? She wants to eat from all of the sections. And she'll be at peace with the man who can provide the best in each of those sections."

3

OBSTACLES

"... There is a mountain in front of you. You can choose to go around it. You can choose to go over it, or you can choose to go through it."

Greg

Self-esteem has everything to do with everything you do.

PBS aired a documentary which featured an African-American doctor whose contribution to the black community was to practice medicine in an inner-city hospital emergency room. There he often not only treated victims of crimes who were really innocent victims of their environment, but he treated the perpetrators also. What struck me was a camera shot of the doctor early one morning after an all-night shift on duty. He can be seen from behind standing just outside of the emergency room entrance, dressed in his surgical scrubs with his arms stretched out to each side. He was probably tired and may have been stretching, looking forward to a restful sleep. But to me, it seemed he was taking in the world rather than a breath of fresh air. He was living his life his way. Because he wanted to, he was repairing the damage from the destruction in the community, as best he could, in his own way. And I thought, at that moment, he must have felt a sense of power and control over himself that many black men and women don't experience. I envied him.

Empowerment, self-esteem, self-love—it all relates to how we interact with others.

When you are considered less, or when your people are considered less, it affects you. It hurts. I watch my 3-year-old nephew run around like a free spirit. King of the world. And it hurts to know that one day he will be forced to realize the limitations that others will attempt to place on him simply because of the color of his skin. Limitations that I don't believe would be placed upon him if he were a white male.

Leo's comments on self-esteem bring to mind what people sometimes say about old age. "You either get old, or you don't." He suggests black men have so much against them, they have no choice but to develop self-esteem or die.

"The reason it's so important is because the black man has so many extraordinary obstacles against him that he's starting the game getting 10 points!" he said. "That's how much of an underdog he is. If he doesn't have any self-esteem, he doesn't have any kind of a shot!"

He said the black man's burden is unique in that he is forced to maintain a delicate balance between his natural mental and physical strengths and the impending defeat that society predicts for him.

"If there were a way a test could be done of different human beings, the black man would be the strongest in the world. The Afro-American black man. Not only is he physically strong in terms of that whole slave thing, but I think mentally and spiritually the brothers have got to put forth so much more of an effort than the average man out there, just in daily life, that I think there is a two-edged sword.

"I think that's why the men who are successful are very successful, but I think that's also why you see so many failures. Because they just can't deal with the bullsh—. The constant day-to-day pressures they receive as black men in America... from everywhere.

"It's so tough that in order for him to have any moderate amount of success, he's got to develop tools or skills that a lot of other ethnic groups might be able to take for granted. Spiritual skills, emotional skills.

"The maturation of a man from the time he's a boy and he deals with life experiences; if he's worth his salt, he's going to have to do things that are going to allow him to be a better individual. Everybody does that. Life has a way of forcing him to do that. So what happens I think in that person's maturation or evolvement, they begin to realize, 'I've got to stay sharp. I've got to be mentally alert. I've got to be able to communicate.' But I think as they get older they realize that they have to develop some kind of spiritual skills. They realize that in order to achieve a high level of peace, they've got to have some kind of belief in something that's superior to them. So I think it's the working or recognition of the task before them that allows them to develop the skills that are going to enable them to [perform and achieve].

"You want to be physically superior, work out. You want to be able to communicate, you go to school, you learn the language, you read. You want to be mentally prepared, you live plainly. You don't drug, you don't drink. You do the things that are going to sharpen your mind. You want to be spiritually correct, you go to church, you pray to whomever that might be for you.

"The point is this whole task of living for me is the continuous task of working with what God gave you. And when it gets to the point where a person says, 'F— it. I'm tired of putting forth the effort,' they are essentially quitting at life."

Adding to Leo's perspective, Greg said men must educate themselves to the hindrances they are going to be forced to deal with. Otherwise they will not be able to overcome them, "Because there is a mountain in front of you. You can choose to go around it. You can choose to go over it. You can choose to go through it. Whatever way is best for you. But the only way to know which way to go is to have that knowledge and know that those ways exist. And then determine which way is best for you. Educate yourself as much as you can."

The positive nature and attributes of a person who is trying to better himself and his life will inevitably be felt by those closest to that person and nearby observers. "The more you can be self-sufficient, the more it's going to build up your self-esteem and self-confidence. It's a chain reaction," Greg continued. " A chain reaction can be positive or negative. If you initiate the positive, hopefully it will get that positive reaction going, people are going to say, 'Oh look at him, he's doing this that or the other. I'd like my son to see him.' [It's important] to notice anyone who is doing something legally, to the best of their ability, with character and pride."

Road blocks are not only in place to hinder black men from going forward. Many have said that before they are given opportunities at the workplace, they must overcome the perception that they cannot succeed. Once that is accomplished they are then required to perform beyond expectations. Greg complained, "We do the same level of work at the same rate as our white counterpart and we're looked upon as average. Whereas they're looked upon as superior. That struggle is always out there and we have to recognize it as a struggle... those are the cards we've been dealt... Now we can play to win or just play to play. I'm playing to win because the people playing against me are definitely playing to win."

Greg and many of the men I talked with only want to be viewed as any other individual, judged on their merit and not by the color of their skin. It hurts and they are sometimes exhausted by it, but day after day they return to the battlegrounds. Greg continued, "They're not playing to lift you up in any kind of way.

You're going to have to lift yourself up." As he said previously, "The only way to do that is to see the situation for what it is and deal with it accordingly."

And "Yes," he said, white people see an aggressive movement of "those of us who see the situation for what it is," and they are threatened by it. But at the same time he wonders, possibly out of hope, why they try to "suppress the push... rather than try to get inside the black man, find out what his problems are and try to help?"

Aliwishes, 60-something, a widowed mother of three, understands the black man's struggle to be the white man, "because he controls the economy and the financial world. He's deciding how the black man is going to live and what kind of life he is going to live. So he knows that he doesn't have that control. And at certain times he has got to do things he doesn't want to do in order to live the way he wants to live. And that might be at the sacrifice of his own ego.

"It can become a problem because he feels frustrated. He can bring that frustration home with him. And if he brings it home to a wife who doesn't realize what he's doing...

"Women don't have their intuition and their sense of insight for nothing. They're suppose to use it. You can tell when something is going on. You can go by his job and see how he is respected or not respected... you can learn everything by observation... You can find out some of the stress that he might be under and learn how to ease it. You have to find out how to deal with it. Find out how to help."

In fact another struggle awaits many men at home, where wives and girlfriends have greater expectations than their employers. Dion, 35, an entrepreneur in Cleveland, said in frustration that his experience has been that the perception of a man is based upon what he can provide. His past loves became impatient when his hard work did not produce immediate results. And he said it's a sad commentary because "... the biggest thing for a man is to know his woman believes in him."

Lou and Dennis faced similar realities in their failed marriages. "A mate should understand what a black man, especially if he's educated, professional, and working in corporate America, goes through," said Lou, 44 of

Baltimore. "He's liable to bring it home. She should know what he is capable of doing and not doing. Instead she compares him to the image she feels he should emulate... that's not fair."

When Lou and his first wife were married, he was juggling a number of political problems at the office while trying to maintain a private business on the side. And as he communicated his troubles to his wife, Lou felt she was not only non-supportive emotionally, but he said, "She used my problems against me..." His voice still filled with disappointment years later, Lou added, "She took me out of the game as far as her role as a teammate and a friend. I couldn't do that to someone I love."

Dennis, 40, of New York, worked for years as a sales executive with IBM, which provided job security and many fringe benefits. He decided to leave IBM and become a stockbroker when he realized in the long run Wall Street could be more lucrative. However, in the beginning he made less money and the financial adjustments became too much for his marriage to withstand. He said his wife had become "accustomed to a certain lifestyle" and it was difficult for her to accept the fact that they could no longer "charge now and pay later." Dining out, vacations, and other perks they had enjoyed while Dennis was with IBM had to become less frequent until he could build his client base.

Dennis and his wife eventually separated and divorced, but he added he could have been more open in discussing the problems they were experiencing. "One of my downsides was my inability to communicate at times," said Dennis. And that coupled with his struggle for success contributed to their marital problems. "I tend to say, 'I can do it myself. I can solve it, just let me deal with it.' "

Black women are tuned in to what black men experience on a daily basis. However, men don't always feel their sensitivity. As Lou commented, many believe the average black woman will compare them to an image of what she believes a man should be, rather than who that individual man is in reality.

Sherry, 33, a corporate attorney in New York, is an insightful, no-nonsense, thought-provoking woman who grasps what black men go through. She does not hold an unrealistic view of what her husband can accomplish. Accommodating the needs that may arise from his struggle is another story.

"A black man must fight to get through life the best he can in a racist world," she said. "They put him in the lowest of categories. And I guess it's different for us, being women and black women, a double minority. It's also a benefit because you don't get conflicting signals from society. On the one hand, you're black and you're not as good. On the other hand, you're a woman. Whether or not you want to see that as being put on a pedestal, or not as good, there is no conflicting signal as to where to direct your attention. You have an expectation that people are going to hit you with one or the other.

"A black man has definite conflicting signals. On the one hand he's black in a white society and he's not as good. On the other hand, he's told he's a man. And as a man he's supposed to provide for his family and be a success.

"So, as a woman, if you don't make very much or you don't get a job offer... you may not get to buy your new clothes. You may not be able to feed your children. It may have very serious consequences. But, it's not, 'You're a failure as a woman,' because society tells you your role is to be a mother, wife, supporter, et cetera. You may rail against that, but that is what society has told you is your role. If a man doesn't achieve that, it's not only that his family doesn't eat... but he also failed as a man.

"It's a conflicting signal because racism tells him he can't and manhood tells him it's his responsibility. All around I think they have it harder than we do."

Leo explained that although Sherry's assessment is correct, every man has the same pressures. "But with black men it's highlighted because the pressure for him isn't necessarily from the expectations he has for himself. It's the expectation that society, his family, his woman, and other ethnic groups have of him. And none of those groups that I just mentioned, when you get down to it, [have] the faith or the belief that he is going to succeed. There is more doubt than anything in my opinion."

It is because of this doubt and expectation that Leo feels the black man's biggest struggle is the black woman. Because she is his "last bastion of hope. His last bastion of security. When he feels like he can't turn to her, he feels like he can't turn to anyone."

Possibly due to the amount of inner strength required to make it through her own daily experiences, there is a limit to how much Sherry will put herself out to express sensitivity toward her husband's needs. To the extent that, "it doesn't take anything off [her] nose," she would probably help him out.

She said, "For example, we get into a cab. I happen to have the money that day, so I intend to pay the cab driver. One out of ten times he might say, 'Just give me the money.' Maybe he's feeling manly that day and he wants to pay. One out of ten times doesn't take anything off me. I'd just think he's having a sudden burst of testosterone. Just give me my change. If it happened all of the time I'd probably become frustrated, but I am sensitive to that kind of thing. I wouldn't like for him to feel diminished as a man. Particularly if it doesn't take any skin off my nose."

She continued, "Some people might say it doesn't matter if you're supportive or not on those occasions. It's the other occasions when it does matter, [when it takes skin off my nose]. Maybe I'm not giving up very much... I certainly don't feel like I am, but there are lots of women who wouldn't even do that."

And those other occasions when it may be necessary for Sherry to put herself out to please her husband? She said they will just have to wait and see.

Regardless of the personal success they attain, black men are pained by the negative perceptions and images of them portrayed in the media. Many believe black women are indifferent to this pain. Among a group of men interviewed, Erroll, a social worker in Atlanta, said, "Women are convinced there are no men out there. And they think the problem is bigger than it is. I think there are more men out there than they want to admit. They're listening to all this hype that says black men are extinct." And the men who are out there are thought to be untrustworthy and irresponsible, and he feels it's "... horribly unfair. I would say you have a bunch of responsible men in this room. But we're never talked about."

Charles, 35, a financial analyst in New York, has known black women who subject him to the same stereotypes that society pins on black men. "Unless you meet someone on very concrete grounds [through a friend or in a professional environment], [stereotypes] are a very hard thing to overcome. There's no reason why I should enter into a relationship with a black woman who believes the black stereotypes."

The same goes for a white woman, but Charles said his experience is "Black women expect black men to be dogs. [Irresponsible] and unfaithful." Admittedly, he said, black men are dogs. "But again that's from my experience... Seeing what my friends do in relationships. And my father. Yes, black men are unfaithful a lot."

"There are some bad brothers and sisters out there," said Greg. "But stop lumping people together. 'Black men are just irresponsible,' 'They just don't have anything going on about themselves,' 'Half of them are in jail or the other half are dead.' Lumping anyone into any category before you know who they are is definitely bad. And we as a people do it to our own. That's the worst of all.

"You kind of expect it from whites, with that fear. It makes them more comfortable if they can just lump all black men together and say, 'Well hell, they're all irresponsible. They're always late. They're never about business...' So we as black men have to fight against that, number one. And then we have to work two to three times harder than our white counterpart."

I have to admit at the start of this project I believed that most black men whom I considered my peers were irresponsible. My experience was I could not depend on them to keep their word or value my heart. And the question of irresponsibility was raised to men with this in mind. I now realize I held an unfair opinion because irresponsibility is not exclusive to any group of people, and I probably impose a heavier burden on the black men I know than I impose on anyone else. "Irresponsibility is not doing the things you have assumed responsibility for," said Leo. "The failure to live up to someone's expectations is not irresponsible. But if I'm going to take on this responsibility and I don't follow through, that's being irresponsible. People must assume responsibility for themselves."

He continued, "How can I expect a black man to take care of a family if he's not taking care of himself in terms of maturation? This whole thing about life is about self-improvement... The only reason black men are cited is because there are so many cases where black men don't take care of their families, which stem from sociological problems..."

"White people have tremendous advantages," Charles said. "White people don't have their sh— together. They just have advantages. White people have terrible relationships. There are more white relationships in this country today than there are black relationships. The reason the white community is not in the same chaos as the black community is because they don't have those barriers that black men and women have to overcome in order to get to neutral and then strive to go ahead... Because this is a white society, white people can afford more chances than a black person to f—- up and then succeed."

4

OBSTACLES
Ain't I a Woman?

That man over there say a woman needs to be helped into carriages and lifted over ditches and to have the best place everywhere.

Nobody ever helped me into carriages or over mud puddles or gives me a best place...

Ain't I a woman?

Look at me... I could work as much and eat as much as a man—when I could get it—and bear the lash as well... and ain't I a woman?

— Sojourner Truth

What is the black woman's struggle?

"Getting the black man, her husband or whoever to appreciate her. To appreciate the efforts she makes.

There are some women who work very very hard and they have all the way back to slavery... So often black men have abandoned the black woman and their children. She has to struggle by herself... There isn't anyone outside of her own children who appreciates what she did...

"Even during the times when women didn't need men and they stayed with them regardless of the drinking or what-ever... through all of that, they never got any credit."

— Aliwishes

Black women struggle too. They have long desired to be acknowledged and have their existence valued at the workplace and at home in their community. The hurt they experience from black men and society is so piercing and so rarely addressed that walls have gone up and whatever inner demons they have, they believe they must face alone.

Women too have their crosses to bear professionally. Every positive action is looked at as extraordinary and every negative action is viewed as typical. But what hurts most is the perception that we are not held in high esteem by our men.

I was in attendance at a forum on young black women and violence, and one of the panelists discussed a previous conversation she had with a white gentleman on the differences in white and black communities. He told her that black men cannot/do not protect their women and families as white men do. He said no one could bring violence and destruction into the white man's community without finding barriers in place to protect their families, unlike the black community, which has no barriers or hindrances in place to protect their women and children. The panelist said she felt the truth of his words and was at a loss as to how to respond to him.

Arguments can be made that white communities are not impenetrable, and that black families protect their children as well as any other community. A black woman may in fact feel safe with her husband or boyfriend, but most women do not feel they are valued by the black male population, much less protected by it. They certainly are aware that the white community is of the opinion that black women are held in low regard by black men. And so they struggle to manage this painful reality without allowing it to defeat them. "You've go to constantly keep stroking and talking to yourself," said Aimee, 32, an interior designer in Atlanta. Survival instinct is what keeps many black women going because "no matter what," she continued, "the children are relying on you. The culture is relying on you. We're the first teachers. We have to be strong."

Often times we are forced to maintain a balancing act and temper our responses because we can't be certain when our emotions and reactions will be intimidating, criticized, or praised. "Being aggressive, outspoken, willing to break the rules and move to the head of the line, it all works very differently in the workplace, " said Rene. One of her struggles is to "learn these games that mother never taught us, so I don't get swallowed up. I'm talking corporate gamesmanship. Because I feel I'm on terrain I never imagined. You should see these white boys play... We don't expect it. The thing is we have to re-examine so much of what it took for us to get where we are."

Many men said they can't help but understand the obstacles black women face. "Just like it's a white man's world," said Charles, "it's a man's world. It's such a male-dominated, oriented world... A black man starts behind the eight ball, but it's just that much more so for a woman. It's hard.

"A woman like Oprah Winfrey isn't given enough credit. I think she's the only black woman ever in the Fortune 400. Men have gone in and out. For a black woman to get where she's gotten is absolutely incredible. She did it based on intelligence and competence. And that is something that is not appreciated a lot in this world."

"Women have suffered just as much, if not more pain than the black male," said Dennis. "Women also have a preconceived notion of themselves that they must conquer," he continued. "Men need to communicate that they understand this situation exists. It doesn't mean men will always understand, but they should concede it exists and be supportive."

Through our mother's eyes many of us grew up seeing inequality and self-denial. But we also learned how they overcame obstacles to survive and get what they wanted. Black men recognize this inner strength, but they hold it against black women when it does not benefit them. And women find they must adapt an interchangeable personality in their relationships. "You must be a man [when the situation calls for it], but still be a woman," said Aimee. "You must be strong and tender... That's the biggest struggle."

Mica, 37, agrees. In a previous relationship, her boyfriend enjoyed her intelligence and outspokenness, but she said it became clear to her over time that he didn't want her to be so overt with him. She said he, as well as her current boyfriend, asked her why she must have an answer all of the time. "They like it when it works to their benefit, but then they develop this, 'Can't you just let me win?' attitude."

To help keep the peace, Mica finds her relationship requires her to be more passive at home, whereas she is direct and demanding at work. And although she's very much in love, she said, "It becomes tiring. I must tone down who I am."

According to Greg, women not only struggle to be a "viable part of our community," they fight to be "a viable part of their relationship." He said, "The worse thing for a strong woman is to have a man who is intimidated by her strength. I definitely want a strong woman. If I'm not around her, she can hold her own. I think everyone wants that. I don't think anyone wants a person in their life who uses them as a crutch."Women must be given the freedom to recognize and assert their strengths. "And as men... we have to nurture it... Whatever they're doing that's right, keep it going."

Anthony, 32, of Rochester, NY, said many men are just uncomfortable with women who, "have their own mind... When a man is in control or with a passive woman, his chest is out. When he has a woman who can relate to something from a different perspective and say, 'No, you're wrong,' it scares him. She becomes intimidating. Especially if she has a lot going on... She's independent and he can't tell her what to do. Many men want that control."

It's the classic case of a person making his problem your problem by projecting their insecurities onto you. I refer to it in my mind as "the stifle," because it can hem you in, almost trap you. At first it's internalized and, depending on the type of person you are, you become either hurt or angry. But it can be subliminal and surface well into a relationship; then you find yourself trying to overcome something that you think common sense can squash, but it's really bigger than you.

When Rene sees the red flag she drops the guy right away. "I had to learn the hard way, through a relationship with a man in my first year of law school... He wasn't very attractive. Folks use to call us 'Beauty and the Beast.' He tore me apart to make himself feel better... I was never pretty enough. I was either too fat or too skinny. When we'd walk down the street he'd point out my inadequacies. He'd sleep with other women and tell me it was my fault. Had I done more of this or less of that, he wouldn't have slept around."

It took Rene two years to regain her self-esteem after the relationship ended. "What I realized in that relationship is that if a man is intimidated by you, he's intimidated because he's insecure. He's afraid of you. And the best thing you can do is get away from that man because he will destroy you."

5

Equality, Prerequisites, & Expectations

Most women consider equality a foregone conclusion in their relationships. But ask a man and "it ain't necessarily so."

"If she wants equality and then expects a suitor to court her, she can't be his equal," said Lou, adding that women are "hypocritical" in wanting a man to pay the tab, be chivalrous, and protect them, as they also demand to be viewed on equal terms. He is more accepting of a concept in which both parties buck societal roles and freely express themselves. Ideally, that is a beautiful concept. But it is not always the reality of what takes place.

I must acknowledge that when I meet a girlfriend for dinner I have no expectations that she will pay for dinner. We meet, have a good time, pay our tabs, and find our respective ways home. When I go out with a man, either a friend or a romantic interest, in the back of my mind I feel he should pay for dinner. I do not necessarily go with the expectation that he is going to pay. In fact, I make sure that I am prepared for him not to. But on a first date especially, my image of him as a gentlemen is based on whether or not he pays for the meal. Consciously or subconsciously, I think to myself, 'If he is a gentleman, he'll take care of it,' because I view the man as the provider. So much so that I feel awkward when I do pay because it is imbedded in me that paying is his responsibility.

Phillip, 39, Norfolk, Virginia, believes, "A man treating a woman like a queen creates a level of expectation in her... Being treated as an equal takes away her specialness." He went on to say, "But she wants to feel great. For example, 'I have my own mind.'"

Opinions like Phillip's place women on the defensive because such behavior is perceived as an effort to control. It suggests that a woman is not free to express her honest views without a negative response. "I'm entitled to my opinion whether I agree with you or not!" said Jenny.

As women of color our psyches don't allow us to believe or accept that it is wrong to be treated unequally among others because we are black, but it is right to be considered unequal among our men because we are women.

"Many black men are out there telling white men they don't want to get their butts kicked just because they are black men," said Rene. "They don't want to be discriminated against just because they're black men. They don't want assumptions made about their intellectual abilities just because they are black men. But then they want to come home and kick our butts just because we're women! No! You must examine the same ideas you are telling white folks to examine about you. And if you're not willing to do that... We're going to have a problem!"

With these beliefs and sensitivities in mind the women interviewed had an "aversion" to the concept of a role in marriage when it pertained to themselves, although they were clear that the role of their mates was that of a loving, supportive partner.

"What's a role!?" Linda said. "Maybe I'm confusing it with duty and I feel I must be dutiful to myself."Linda, 35, explained that her grandmother raised her, but throughout most of her childhood and teenage years she experienced a sort of role reversal. She was the caretaker of her household, which also included her brother. As her grandmother got older it was Linda's duty to "dress her, wash her back, tie her shoes, et cetera... I couldn't go away to school because my grandmother needed me there with her." She said in a marriage or partnership there is a mutual role, "... of love, support, listening, communication. To treat each other special. Help each other financially. Both parties should contribute unless there is an agreement for example that, one will not work, because he or she is going to school... Otherwise I don't believe in supporting a man."

"I still don't understand," Linda continued. "Is there a special role? [Yes], to be sensitive to the fact that he is the most feared. But don't put down what I want to achieve!"

Cathy, 30, a corporate attorney in New York, has an ongoing argument with her father over the role of men and women within their relationships. "I like to think there is no defined role for either person," she said, "and things get worked out couple by couple. [Still], when I want someone to carry my groceries up the stairs or take out the garbage, I tell my boyfriend, 'That's a man's job.'"

Cathy's father raised her and her sister to expect equality with their relationships. As adults they are now being advised "the man should have the last word." She said, "[My father] shocked me when he said that. He says, 'You can contribute what you think, but somebody has to have the last word. And it should be the man because he has it so hard in the world that he should be able to make decisions in his own household.'

For Aimee, loving supportive partners are able to be an emotional rock for each other. "When times get hard... sometimes before money, before any type of bail-out, you need that emotional... stability... that security blanket. Because sometimes that is all you have. You feel if somebody else is there, you can do anything. Sometimes all you need to know is that somebody is in your corner."

Conscious of differing expectations, Cathy is content that she is involved with someone "who is not rigid in [his] definition of roles in the relationship and is open-minded to how those roles may interchange."

Usually her boyfriend provides the emotional support and strength she needs from him. "In a crisis, he's not as good," she said. "He gets very nervous. Like last month. This was a really horrible month at work. I was working around the clock... hating the assignments I was working on. I was upset. I would come home and just cry for two hours. And he would just say, 'Call your sister! Call your mother!' [At midnight], I'd say, 'No, I can't call anyone, it's your job to help me through this!' "Simply not knowing how to help her in this type of crisis, Cathy's boyfriend would ask her, "'Don't you have any friends that are still up? You have to call somebody. I can't deal with this!' "

Men desire loving, supportive partners, too. They see themselves as "the providers," but many said ideally they would like a balance with their mates to offset each other's strengths and weaknesses.

Although Dennis is not always successful in implementation, he sees his role as one of guidance. "The man should create the atmosphere for the family to survive and thrive. He should be the provider. He doesn't have to dominate, but he should lead when his strengths call for it. He should concede that leadership when the woman's strengths demand it."

"I look at it as you and I against the world," said Greg. "Whatever it takes to keep you strong, that's the role I need to assume. And vice versa. I would hope my significant other would assume that role... We basically work off each other."

Raisa, 42, a pharmaceutical saleswoman in Connecticut, wants to be romanced at the beginning of her relationships. "Court me. Be punctual. Be honest in answering questions. Be generous, romance me and be patient, you'll get yours. Don't give me less when you can give more. Don't bring over beer because you like it, when you can bring a nice wine instead." And most importantly, Raisa said, "Show interest. Sometimes when I'm out with a man I get tired of injecting things about myself because he's so busy talking about himself. I get tired of having to reminding him that I'm here too... 'There's another person over here!' I just get tired of having to fight to be heard. I'd like it if occasionally there was an interest in me and I was asked a few questions about myself."

Rene has experienced similar frustrations and she becomes annoyed when she is in the company of men who have little interest in her knowledge or opinions, "In the past I put on a certain level of unintelligence to make them feel more comfortable... I'd sit there and nod and smile and say, 'Yeah, I can see that... you're right.' Just so I wouldn't make them feel uncomfortable. I don't do that anymore. Now if they say something stupid... I'll correct them. And if they can't handle it... if they're intimidated and I can see that... I drop them immediately."

As a photographer surrounded by models, Greg prefers a woman who is down to earth. "In my business I deal with a lot of people who are starting to believe their hype... They expect men to grovel and put them on some pedestal. I don't have time for that. I don't buy into it. If you want to project a certain attitude for the purpose of the photo session, fine. Diva, bitch, whatever... but once the session is over, just be real.

"I want a woman who can feel comfortable around my friends. My friends are not pretentious, they are just good people. I want a person I can take around my peers and colleagues and feel that she can intelligently hold her own. And at the same time if I want to take her down home to my relatives, she can eat collard greens and corn bread with her fingers and feel comfortable doing that. Just be real. That's the only prerequisite that I have. You don't have to look a certain way or have any particular amount of money... If you can't come down here and sit and talk without feeling that you're beneath this situation, I don't need it."

"I expect her to allow me to know her," said Anthony 33, of Rochester, NY. "She has to let me know if she's content or if there's something that needs to be discussed. If you like a man, why should you let him go just because he didn't do this or that? Hell, maybe the brother didn't know. Maybe you learned something he didn't learn. Maybe you need to teach him."

Anthony's comments reflect a feeling among many men that women lay the burden of the relationship on men, expecting them to be aware of their needs as well as resolve any conflicts single-handedly. And when the relationship inevitably fails, the men are believed to be at fault.

"Communication opens everything," Anthony continued. "Words are [commitment]. They commit us once we share what's on our minds. When we don't communicate, we're both at fault. And when we're both working at communicating, we're [expressing] what we mutually feel and want."

In marriage women expect and hope their husbands remain sensitive to their needs, remain committed, and be a "real partner in raising children." Although many grew up in two-parent households, their mothers carried the weight of child-rearing. "If I'm home with the children all day," said Shayla of Rochester, NY, "when he gets home I need someone I can talk to on my level."

Finola, 32, requires only "general support and attention" from her husband to be content. "I don't have many expectations whereas he has too many... I'm generally happy when he is happy and growing. I'm bad about addressing my needs."

Leo went into his second marriage with different expectations than his first marriage. "My primary expectation was being in something that was manageable." He felt his previous marriage required him to be more accountable than he cared to be. "I wanted a woman that was independent and secure enough in herself to realize how I am, that I literally wasn't willing to compromise at all. I was very selfish."

In his first marriage to Angela he thought he could handle all of their problems by himself. "I always felt it was my role to not only try to juggle my sh—, but say, 'Come on baby, just put your sh— right on my back, too. You know I can carry you.' "

Finding no reward in that behavior, Leo said he went into his second marriage expecting more of a fifty-fifty partnership. He has discovered that his wife's sense of security has allowed him to be himself at all times and in return he is very accommodating to her.

He said selfishness is a thin line. "I'm extremely flexible, but it's because she has been so accommodating. You know, men always feel a sense of having to prove themselves to women. And they will do anything to prove themselves. That's why I think I'm a man for the 21st century, because I don't feel I've got to prove sh— to a woman. No more than what I ask her to prove to me.

"I remember when I was younger and the whole sex thing was of such significance to me that I would do almost anything to please a woman. Not necessarily because I wanted to, but because I felt I had to. Now I'm just a lot more comfortable. I may not feel like lying up f— all night and sweating and cramping. I may not feel like having oral sex with her until my jaws feel like they are about to drop off, because she demanded her orgasm. 'I'll throw in the towel, coach—I quit. I'm out of the game.'

"I have no problems assuming that role... because, you know what? Hakeem Olajuwan has had bad games. Nobody's f—-g with him because he's had a bad game. Why does my woman gotta be George Steinbrenner every f—-g time we go to bed?

"I'm much more comfortable now. The sex thing doesn't hold for me the whole [appeal] that it use to... I don't feel like I have to do for a woman financially because she's a woman... I think more than ever, I treat women as people."

With that in mind, what expectations does Leo's wife have of him? "I know she has a strong sense of security," he said. "She wants me to be the best husband, the best father, the best man I can be. I don't think she expects me to shortchange myself. And I think she realizes if I do shortchange myself, then I'm going to shortchange her."

6

Kalieding

"I think it's fairly obvious there is a problem," said Leo. "Black women just don't think that black men really understand them, no matter how well you articulate it. There are a lot of black women that I know who are very lonely and can't find black men or can't get along with black men. And I know a lot of black men who for whatever reason can't get along with black women, but they aren't as lonely."

They aren't as lonely because they will turn to women of other ethnic backgrounds more often than black women will turn away from black men and towards men of other races. Sherry theorized that if women limit themselves to available black men, the ratio imbalance "makes men arrogant about their prospects. Why shouldn't they be if the ratio is two to one? They can afford to be more selective."

In her mind it is no different than any other aspect of life. "It's just like if you graduate from Yale Law School. You don't have to go to just any law firm and hang out your shingle. You have your choice of lots of different opportunities.

"Their actions are just natural human behavior. If you have lots of options before you... of course you are going to take the opportunity and explore them. It's only when people decide they are going to settle down that they realize there is no benefit to behaving in that manner."

"I truly believe that everybody wants a loving relationship," said Greg. "A lot of women have that attitude of, 'All he wants is sex. Keep it away and he'll be here. But as soon as I give of myself then the whole tide has turned. He's in control.' I don't believe that. But if you approach men from that perspective, then your actions are going to reflect that type of thinking. And that man is going to pick up on it.

"He might want you as a person. But if you are going to dangle sex out there in front of him, 'can't have none of this until you do this,' then it becomes a conquest. Then [for him] it becomes, 'Well, as soon as I get this, then I'm going to show you some things.' Then the possible relationship has been tainted, simply because she was thinking, 'All he wants is sex anyway, so I just need to use this sex as bait to make him do what I want him to.'

"There are situations when it is a physical thing. And I think that goes for men as well as women. That's not all men are after, believe it or not. Every man is not trying to jump your bones and lay you down."

The needs men express seem reasonable to me. So why do we have such problems getting it together? I know that I am more than capable of being a supportive partner. I went through a long, frustrating period in which my interaction with men never reached a point where we could become aware of each other's capabilities. It seemed we could not get past first base, to a place where they could get to know me or I could get to know them.

And yet initially they seemed so interested.

"Somebody is lying," said Anthony in reply to why men and women have problems if they are searching for the same things. "If we realize we want each other, everything outside of that we're going to have to work at and talk about." He continued, "It's not just going to fall into place. The only thing that's going to fall into place is what you and I are giving to each other. But as soon as you're not giving or we're both taking, we don't have a relationship. It's gone."

Eddie and I went out after two months of checking each other out at the volunteer center. "Hopefully this is the beginning of something special and I think we should be up front with each other," he said. During dinner on our second date he began to tell me about his past, which included a period of trouble with the law. He said he wanted to pre-empt someone else telling me first.

When we spoke over the following days, he always mentioned his desire for quality time over the coming summer months. My mother was due in town soon for a visit and he wanted to meet her. Everything was great... and then I invited him over one night after he finished work. My intention was to show him some of the work I was doing on the book. He arranged to get off early so he could see me "as soon as possible."

The moment he entered the doorway we were entwined, but I was also upset. I had phoned my mother before he arrived and something was terribly wrong with her. Later that evening, when she was okay, we discovered she had a reaction to medication her doctor had given her. But while the reaction was in effect, I didn't know what to think. I feared she was having a stroke and I felt totally helpless. I needed emotional support.

Eddie left.

He was allergic to my cat, but it was just as well because he was only interested in one thing. He said, "I'll call you as soon as I get home." I left him a message shortly after, letting him know my mother was okay. I didn't hear from him until three days later and I haven't seen him since.

Looking back, I know I was fortunate that it was only a brief interaction. But at the time I liked him, I was interested in pursing a relationship, and I couldn't understand his change in behavior. Today I speculate that during our brief time he could clearly see the type of person I was and what he could expect, but he wanted something else.

Then there was Derek. We met one night at happy hour. We had lots of chemistry, my weakness. We spent hours together talking about how we felt about life. When our dates ended it always felt as if we had left a part of ourselves with each other. Which means you can feel enriched from what you've experienced and at a loss because it's ended.

Problem No. 1: Derek lived with someone. Following a nice dinner, a long walk, and hours of conversation the night we met, he gave me the wrong telephone number. After some discussion over his failure to be forthcoming with that information, I made the decision to see him anyway.

Problem No. 2: I brought up his significant other. Derek mentioned his relationship on a few occasions, but he was never very specific. I wanted to know the deal. Did he love her? Was he going to marry her? What's the problem? Where is this going with us?

I didn't walk away from that conversation with any concrete answers. He told me he didn't want to do anything to destroy what we had, which he was usually prone to do.

Until that point he had been very attentive, reliable, and consistent. Then everything changed: he became the opposite. What disappointed me most was he was never straight with me. He'd say he would call, knowing he probably wouldn't or he'd cancel our plans at the last minute, always providing a rational explanation. Finally one day we had arranged to get together and I phoned him at his office in the morning to schedule the time. He said he'd call me back, but I never heard from him.

Some men have suggested that once a man learns what he is going to get or not going to get out of the situation, he acts accordingly. That could mean stepping off.

"Sometimes men play roles to get what they want, knowing that once they reach a plateau, he must make a decision to go forward or not. And when the pressure hits him, he realizes he must front after using manipulation to get what he wanted." said Anthony.

The problems men and women face while interacting go way beyond sex. Everyone seems so caught up in their own struggles. It's either a "damn anyone who gets in my way" mindset or they never have the consideration to look up and deal with what is in front of them. Trust, respect and consideration have disappeared and selfishness has taken their place. This is true among men and women.

Almost everyone interviewed acknowledged without hesitation that they have difficulty trusting others, even their mates. I must include myself in that group. However, an inability to trust is nothing to be proud of.

Kenny, married three years said, "I don't ever trust to the point that if she waivers, if she violates that trust, I suffer."

I asked him if that attitude creates a negative cloud over his marriage. He said, "No. I'm doing all that should be done and at the same time hedging myself. If my expectations aren't achieved, I don't lose much."

Finola, married two years, said she has to trust her husband to some degree because they live apart a great deal of the time. "But I'm no fool. I was raised to believe you don't trust men."

If you have been betrayed or taken advantage of, it can be difficult to determine when to let someone back in. That difficulty sometimes manifests itself into selfishness.

Josh and I had a lot to deal with under normal circumstances, let alone the under the additional crises in his life. I had what felt like a mountain of insecurities left over from a previous long-term relationship, which affected my self-esteem. My writing aspirations, which began before we met, had resulted in an unorthodox work schedule that Josh found unsettling. He would have preferred that I work Monday through Friday, nine to five like "most people," and his failure to meet the goals he set for himself at his job also upset him.

My relationship with his daughter, Lisa, went from mutual affection to little or no affinity on her part, probably due to mismanagement of our interaction. It seemed we were thrown together with almost no prior notice. As an adult, I found it uncomfortable because I generally like to know what lies ahead of me. I imagine it was also uncomfortable for her, a child who was still feeling me out, in her own way, in addition to feeling possessive of her Dad. She developed understandable feelings of resentment. I would have felt the same way with my father.

It came as no surprise one day when Josh casually alluded to her resentfulness. To him it was surprising, flattering, and cute. I felt hurt, treated like an unimportant non-issue to be placed on the back burner until he saw fit to reunite Lisa and I. What intensified it for me was the fact that my family's and friends' children are a natural part of my life and in this case I felt like a rejected outcast.

Separately, it was obvious to me that Lisa's mother, who was married and not the other party in his previous relationship, pulled Josh's strings too easily and on a consistent basis. Although I had not been directly affected yet, I knew in the future it would become a problem that I would have to reckon with.

These issues, compounded by the death of Josh's brother and his continued mourning over the break of his previous relationship, were a lot for Josh and our relationship to bear.

A friend of ours told him that in the space of only a few months he had to endure three of life's most difficult dilemmas: the loss of a loved one, a major change in a committed relationship, and instability or uncertainty at the workplace. Shutting down was the only way Josh knew how to cope.

As he withdrew, I reached out. I hoped his withdrawal was temporary. I gave him space and let him know I was there if he needed me.

A few months later I was talking with a friend while trying to maintain some type of optimism. I asked her how she overcame her cautious nature and survived the difficulties she and her fiancee endured early on in their relationship. She said at some point you must have faith. You have to just trust and believe in the person you are with.

I believed in him. I knew God loved him. The grace of God was with him through the loss of his brother. That awareness kept me in the relationship while few to none of my needs were fulfilled.

More time passed. With every show of support, Josh withdrew further. Finally, after I decided to remain in the so-called relationship through the Christmas holidays, I entered a self-imposed positive state of mind. As a gift from my heart for Josh, I framed the words to the song, "I Believe in You and Me." The words were only a statement of love, not demands. He read it carefully, closed his eyes, and was then non-responsive. He didn't even say, "Thank you." This crushed me, and it was the end for us.

I learned from his past actions that Josh didn't know how to receive my type of love or respond to it, even if he wanted to. However, that does not excuse his insensitivity to me.

Josh later acknowledged that he knew he had no intention of fulfilling any of the needs I expressed to him, not even on the occasions that he pleaded with me not to push him away. Occasions when he knew I was ready to let go. But he said he was in a fragile state, trying to work through other issues. "Just don't push me away!" he said. And suddenly I couldn't, because I loved him.

The thing is, while it was true he was in a fragile way, he did not need me because he wanted me or loved me. He couldn't bear the rejection and he wanted me to continue to be around for him, even if it was at arm's length, which is where he kept me. He wanted me there for him so he could hold on to his sense of equilibrium.

Webster's Dictionary defines selfishness as, "Caring only or chiefly for oneself; concerned with one's own interests, welfare etc. regardless of others; manifesting concern only for oneself." You cannot give everything you have to someone and keep nothing for yourself. Mental, physical and spiritual health is essential to life and survival. However, some things to an extreme, can be a bad thing.

The Benefit of the Doubt

How do you move on, and in fairness, give the next person the benefit of the doubt?

"How much benefit of the doubt do you give him!?" commented Tina about Robert, a longtime friend of mine. After several months of telephone conversations and a brief time together when I was visiting friends in his town, we agreed to slowly pursue our attraction. But suddenly Robert was unreachable and did not return my phone calls.

"I don't give anybody the benefit of the doubt," said Tina. When the right one comes along, she believes she'll know it instinctively and she'll give him the benefit of the doubt.

In agreement, Cynthia said, "She's right. You don't give no black man the benefit of the doubt. A white man maybe. But a black man? Uh-uh."

Starting out with a clean slate is difficult for many, especially women. "A lot of women shut down," said Aimee, "because they know every time they give a little, they're going to get suckered. There's no gray area for a lot of women. They either give of themselves or they don't give at all.

"A lot of women go into a relationship giving 150 percent. You don't know how to give anything less. And you come across a lot of men who flip the script. And instead of seeing a sweet, decent, respectful, loving, giving woman, they see sucker, easy, take advantage. And they will try it. I've been there."

"We can't let our past experiences dictate our attitudes toward who we deal with or how we deal with people in the future," said Greg. "Yes, keep it in the back of your mind, don't forget it. Usually there are signs this is about to be a bad situation... At the same time you have to be objective towards the new person, so give them the benefit of the doubt until they give you reason not to."

Still, in reality it is a struggle. I'm learning to be true to myself, which enables me to have peace of mind. I am pretty agreeable and accommodating if I know what's going on. But when I don't know what's up, I don't have peace of mind.

When I was at a loss as to why I had not heard from Robert, Linda gave me grief about the three calls I had made to him. *"Honey,"* she said, *"you've already called two or three times more than I would have... Maybe you were friends, but your relationship has taken on a new aspect. I would let him reach out to me."* I tried not to feel low after her comments, but I did.

I awoke on Sunday morning less than a week later thinking of him. He had appeared in my dream and he seemed troubled. Knowing I wouldn't be able to shake him all day, I tried to reach him again. He answered the phone. He really gave me a lot of bull——, no true explanation of why I hadn't heard from him. And then he blew me off and said he'd call me later, which of course he didn't.

I was disappointed, but not as disappointed as I had been over the weeks since we had spoken and seen each other. I had given him the benefit of the doubt and I discovered that he was not what I was searching for.

As a friend, he had more knowledge of me and my feelings than a new acquaintance. And yet despite whatever transpired in his life, he did not have the respect and consideration to call and at least offer a brief explanation that he may be out of touch. I said to myself, "Now I know. I may not know why, but I know that he is not what I'm searching for."

Weeks later our mutual friend Brian shed light on the difficulties that Robert was experiencing and how he tends to manage his crises. Brian said Robert often withdraws from everyone he would normally communicate with even though it is understood that they will be his support system in times of need.

He said Robert is not one who will manipulate, intentionally hurt, or say one thing and mean another; he's very direct. If he appears all over the place, there's something going on, a crisis on the horizon. Then Brian went on to explain some of the inner turmoil that Robert was experiencing.

I appreciated what he told me. It made me more sensitive to Robert. I cared about him. However, I also had a feeling of indifference or nonchalance, because I still couldn't understand why, regardless of how "he manages his crises," he couldn't overcome them just enough to phone me and leave a message saying, "I'm going through chaos, madness et cetera... I just wanted to touch bases, I may not be in touch for a while."

Robert and I had had endless conversations over my struggling relationship with Josh. He was aware of my sensitivities and how I tried to hold on when there was nothing to hold on to. He always advised me to "Give the brother the benefit of the doubt," knowing in reality, there was probably no benefit to be had. But he'd say, "You never know what a person is going through."

He was aware of my desire for consideration from a man. We had revisited a conversation when I was in town, about a night that Josh had called unexpectedly asking to come over and spend the night. He said he just wanted to crash, but I was insulted by the phone call. We no longer had that type of relationship. Josh didn't return my calls following that night and we didn't talk directly for several weeks. Robert suggested maybe it was true that all Josh wanted to do was crash. Robert had been in that situation. My opinion was that even if he was sincere and I was wrong in my assumptions, didn't I warrant the benefit of the doubt, consideration, and a phone call?

So there I was once again faced with someone saying "f—- you" to what I might think or how I might feel. In my mind Robert was saying, "What I'm going through is too enormous to think about you. I'll make it up later, if at all."

Everyone has their own personal struggles in life. When they become involved in a relationship they also have their own personal intentions or agenda. Reconsideration of how that agenda is implemented and an active concern for the other party is in order. Our actions are internalized by the people in our lives and create the negative perceptions that are expressed within these pages. Negative perceptions can fester and result in a chain reaction where a person may feel they've been misled, so they will mislead. If little regard has been give to them, they will give little regard to others.

7

"It's A War Out There!"
Leo

eo contends there is a war—not a battle, but a war—between black men and women and every aspect of their relationships is rooted in this truth. "Black women want what they want. Black men want what they want. And everything," he says, "is an offshoot of that. All levels of compromise. All levels of trust. All levels of interaction are based on two aspects of their nature." The woman's desire for security and the man's desire for sex. "And from those two positions everyone is jostling and trading for position to get what they want."

Black women seem to put themselves at a disadvantage in many ways, but mainly because "most have an allegiance to black men." When interacting, "They deal with a black man with an eye towards the possibility of some type of permanency... and they aren't true to themselves or him about what they really want or need." They want to love and to be loved and cared for by a black man, which is automatically a self-imposed limitation.

Black women also approach their relationships with black men with caution and suspicion thinking, "All this brother wants to do is f— me and go on about his way." Cognizant men, he said, are "fed up" with the process they must go through with sisters and "the trade off they offer brothers in terms of the premium they put on their sex... Look, quite frankly, it makes sense to me. If a black woman sees a black man with an eye toward him being a partner, she thinks he's not going to want someone who is sexually uninhibited. So I think it's only natural that she's going to put limits on that aspect of her personality.

"It becomes frustrating because she imposes more limits than probably any other woman out there." Unlike most black women, black men leave their options open. For instance, Leo adds, "If you're dealing with a white woman, both parties do it without the expectation of falling in love. There's no expectation or eye toward permanency. It's sex. Now if it blossoms into something, that's great. But there isn't that cloud of, 'I've got to lock this motherf—-ker up.' "

Most black women believe a black man can find the character traits he is searching for in a black woman. If he wants a passive woman, he can find a black woman who is passive. If he wants a freak, he can find a black woman who is a freak. If he wants a dominating woman, he can find that, too. He is choosing to be with a white woman instead of a black woman.

Leo says we are forgetting, "Men want to f——." And men who "opt" for white women, particularly, "black men of wealth, find the woman who most often satisfy their needs." It's not that black women won't fulfill their needs, with pleasure, "but you've got to go through the whole process with them and it's much more extensive than with the white woman. [Black women] have more inhibitions. They have more morals... A higher code of ethics.

"It's a war! Men are jockeying to f——. Women are jockeying for security...and each party is doing everything they can to achieve their objective. They're lying. They're stealing. They're being irresponsible. They're generating myths... They will do anything."

And black men should not be blamed for all of the casualties from this so-called war. "Black women," says Leo, "must take responsibility for themselves. They don't take responsibility."

Yet he believes they've got the power. He went on, "They're in the position of saying yes or no because they've got what men want. But they get confused [and perhaps shirk their responsibility] with their inability to realize they are made up of so much more than just p——y. And because a man might want that it, it isn't the essence of [women] totally as a people."

Leo's words capture an internal struggle some black women have that white women are not burdened with. "White women have always been very sure about their position as it relates to society and men. Black women have never had that kind of freedom. They're just beginning to realize the sort of freedoms they have as women and as black women." As black women feel their oats through society, and sexually, they must discover where they fit in with black men and white men. History and the perception of black women that arose from the rapes and sexual abuse sustained in slavery, mixed with any lifetime abuse, haunt black women on the most subtle levels.

Women enjoy sex, too. It's not her "p——y" that she's protecting, it's her inner self. Because she knows if the sex is good, she's going to want more, and soon her emotions, not her head, are going to play an increasing role in the relationship.

A woman may relinquish her power early on by allowing the guy to direct and control the ebb and flow of the relationship. He may want to spend every free minute she has together. He may want to just take her in like there's no tomorrow. "There's nothing like new p—-y," said Leo. But when the excitement wears off, distractions may steer his attention in other directions. And he is blamed for the sudden change when she wasn't an active participant in the first place.

"When a woman lets go of the things that are most important to her, she gives up who she is. It's a major turning point in the relationship. It is then his world and it is hard for her to get it back." That was Phillip's opinion when we discussed whether men are aware of the point when a woman may let go of her power or personal responsibility in a relationship.

Personal responsibility extends well beyond the common scenario presented. Women know but don't always heed the fact that there is a fine line within themselves between being empowered and being powerless, devalued, and degraded. Ending up on the wrong side of the line is not, in many cases, the result of another person. It can be due to a woman's miscalculation of her integrity, a gamble with her cahoonas, or a test of her sexual boundaries. Being on the wrong side of the line can be a devastating feeling because she gave up her empowerment, she wasn't robbed of it. She may, however, be exploited by it.

This line in a woman is comparable to the male ego—fragile. And when she gambles or risks her integrity, or explores her soul, it is her responsibility to be with someone she trusts and who values her.

Greg discussed a young woman who took a dangerous risk during Freak-nik Weekend in Atlanta. His photography studio and apartment face the main strip that cars cruise at night. He said, "One night about eleven there was bumper-to-bumper traffic... I saw this girl in a car with about three or four other girls. She decides she wants to get out of the car, and she gets up on the hood and starts dancing.

"Now mind you, there are mobs of guys just roaming all around. Everyone caught up in the excitement. As people drive by, guys might say, 'Show that ass! Show that ass!' Because it's Freak-nik, there was unabashed sexuality running around.

"Anyway this girl gets up on the car and starts dancing. She's just shaking and dancing, and all of a sudden the guys start yelling 'Show that ass! Show that ass!' She turns around and lifts up her dress and shows her behind...And these guys went berserk. They snatched her down and ripped off her clothes...

"This was just like a feeding frenzy you've seen on National Geographic... When they finished, this girl had on nothing but her shoes. She had had on one of those little baby doll dresses with briefs or shorts underneath... they were popping her on the behind. And I'm sure they were putting their hands inside of her.

"Her girlfriends are in the car, just shocked! They start blowing the horn and trying to run over people to get them off the girl. It was just crazy!"

I asked how she was when she got up. He continued, "She was just in shock. Just looking like, 'I can't believe they just swarmed me like this.' One minute she was on top of the car dancing, the next instant she was down on the hood of the car on her stomach, with her face pressed against the windshield and they were ripping off her clothes. She was doing her best to fight them off, but this was sixty to seventy guys. It was late, traffic was not moving. They were all just popping her... Finally as the girl behind the wheel started going forward, she got back in. I could see her face and she was just shaking.

"A guy gave her the t-shirt off his back because she was totally nude except for her shoes. Guys were running around waving her clothes in the air like they were a trophy...

"That type of baiting situation is not good. Sexually baiting a man is not good. Women feel like a man should be able to suppress and control that type of thing. True enough, he should, but don't bait him and you don't have that situation to deal with."

Still in disbelief over the incident, Greg added that men are always responsible for their actions. "But a woman needs to be accountable for her actions also... Men are sexual creatures. We act and react to the physical." In an intimate situation between two people, he continued, "You know what you want and what you don't want. You can let it be known in no uncertain terms— 'Look, I like you. I like being with you, but we're not about to be physically intimate.' You can express that to a man in a way where you don't have to be hostile or condescending. But don't allow an intimate situation to manifest itself and then think that at the drop of a hat a man is going to say, 'Well hey, cool, no problem. Just forget it.' I think that can present a problem that no one wants to deal with.

"I'm sure we've all been in situations where we've been told one thing, but we knew the person really meant something else. That gray area, that area of confusion, is what can springboard you from a real civil, nice, intimate situation, to one that is almost violent. Because the man is thinking, 'Well, she really doesn't mean no. She's just saying no. She really wants me to keep going.'

"We are ultimately responsible for our actions, but women need to know they are ultimately responsible for their actions, too. Just because a man makes a mistake, that doesn't free a woman from all guilt."

"You have women that say, 'Stop, stop. Oh, but let me get that button for you,' " said Jenny during a separate discussion in Atlanta. "And men get confused by that. I think as a woman you are responsible for your own actions. If I go meet a man at two in the morning, I know what I'm going to do. If I took everything off and he's got everything off and I changed my mind... I put myself in that position. I would probably feel like I took it too far and that's the end of it... and if he just went ahead and took it, then I have to go home and realize I messed up."

Years ago, while I was in college, I met a guy one night at Mr. V's, an Atlanta nightclub. We exchanged telephone numbers and we went out a few days later. He drove me to his house, which seemed pretty far. Driving along the dark roads, something told me to make a mental note of the directions in the event I had to leave suddenly. "Where is the nearest main road and pay phone?" I thought. We had a pleasant time at his home. We had a few glasses of wine, watched a little television, and he later took me back to campus. Again I made a mental note for some reason: "The portable TV could easily be in the bedroom next time."

Sure enough, a few days later when he brought me over it was in the bedroom. He had been drinking quite a bit. The next thing I knew he was on top of me, attempting to force me to submit. I was in disbelief that this guy was actually trying to do this against my will! I thought, "I'm out here in the middle of nowhere and he's trying to rape me!" I was using a great deal of strength to fight him, but I was reluctant to go into reserve or scream or bite and scratch because I didn't know how he would react. He was drunk. Finally as he began to enter me he stopped when he realized I was just laying there, non-responsive. He got up and I told him to take me home. He drove a Corvette and I was terrified that we were going to be completely crushed in an accident because of his erratic driving. It seemed liked we just missed the highway guardrail several times. I thought if I was lucky we'd make it within a familiar distance of campus and I'd get out of the car. The whole night made me numb. When we were finally close enough, I got out of the car, slammed the door, and tried to put it all behind me.

I ignored my intuition and placed myself in a situation that could have been potentially much worse than it was. I felt I was at such a disadvantage that the only way I could get out of there was to submit. Fortunately, he stopped.

Crossing the Line

If I were faced with that college situation today, I'm not certain how I would handle it. I feel much more capable of taking care of myself. At the same time, I'm not stupid. But most of the time I don't have a sense or a fear of a man's physical superiority over me. Men say that is precisely many women's problem in relationships. Women don't realize how easily a man can physically react in a volatile situation, and yet they will "dare a man," "jerk his chain," "push his buttons."

Men said women will cross a line that men don't cross with each other without being aware that it will likely cause a violent reaction. Charles has always maintained his self-control, but he said, "Women will push the envelope... Just like you said, men hold back because they know the repercussions. Women will test that... [They will] challenge your manhood and your ability to be a father."

"I hear women talking about, 'Well, he better not hit me,' " said Greg. "And they continuously egg him on. They needle him. And they know his weakness and they try to exploit it. There is nothing worse than being weak in an area and then having the woman who is supposed to be close to you try to exploit that weakness.

"If I had a problem being around strangers and my girlfriend made light of that insecurity, [making] fun of it every opportunity she got, eventually it would cause some type of reaction in me. Maybe a verbal reaction. Maybe I decide not to deal with her. Or I may have a violent reaction. You just never know. Women need to know there are some things you just don't do.

"Women always dare a man. That's what kills me. 'Oh, he ain't going to hit me... he better not hit me, I'll kick his ass.' Many a woman has gotten her ass whipped with that same thought in mind. You don't push men, you don't push anybody because you never know what their breaking point is."

"Pushing" a man might be.

*Driving around town with a man in the car your boyfriend bought for you.

*Going to the club with your boyfriend and attempting to leave with another man.

*Allowing your man to fully support you and then flaunt another love in his face.

*Getting in your man's face in the middle of a heated exchange.

*Getting in your man's face in the middle of a heated exchange and then belittling him.

Women usually have instincts in these type of situations that let us know the potential dangers involved. Red flags were all over a short-lived relationship with Rodney. We'd often go from intimate conversations to explosive shouting matches in seconds. I never understood it, except he always complained that I was holding back mentally, emotionally, and physically. It didn't matter that he was not giving what he demanded of me.

One night we were at his apartment relaxing and enjoying each other. He was partially lying on top of me on the couch. While caressing and talking, he mentioned once again that despite my passion, he wanted more. I told him I was confused, because the day before he told me he had decided to "pull up" on our physical relationship and not place so much urgency and importance on every need. He paused... and then exploded. He told me I was a trip! Selfish! Closed! That I only cared about what made me happy! I screamed back at him while trying to make sense of how our conversation had escalated to this point.

And then I looked at him and I realized that, regardless of the big picture, this guy was livid. He was walking around in circles, ranting on and on about what my problem was. And I knew that it was in my hands to diffuse the situation or continue to argue to the point where he would possibly hit me. The threat was staring me square in the face. It was my turn to pause... and he suddenly looked hurt. I walked over to him and embraced him and we calmed down.

Many women understand and agree with what men have said on this issue. But others don't want to look beyond their insistence that a man should never hit a woman. "My boyfriend was trying to explain this to me," said Cathy. "We had a big fight about it actually. I ended up having to scream, 'Just never speak to me again, unless you can come back and tell me that it's never right!' "

Let me be clear—in my mind it is never okay for a man to be violent with a woman. But in a heated argument a woman must be realistic. She has control over her actions, and his reactions are really beyond her control. Therefore she must act responsibly.

8

The Complexities of Black and White

Upon learning of the development of this book, white men and women assumed the subject matter—problems within relationships between black men and women—meant "The black man's obsession with white women and the black woman's hysteria over it." The truth is interracial relationships are a sensitive area for everyone. Many black women are trying to rid themselves of the hostility they have felt over them. "I look at myself," said Raisa, "I haven't dated in two years and I feel however love comes, if it is something that feels good and it's not harming anyone, go for it. Because love is so hard to find and so hard to keep. Anyone who has true love, God bless them. Interracial relationships are so difficult. Two people must really love one another to enter into that type of union, because you not only have to deal with your own personal issues, you have to deal with society and the many people out there who don't want to accept you."

Intellectually, many women agree. When they see a black man with a white woman their heads tell them it doesn't matter, but their hearts tell them something else. "Whenever I see it I have an involuntary response. It's a guttural jolt to my system," says one woman. "Black men intentionally cast black women aside and seek white women and never admit it. When addressed they use weak excuses like black women are materialistic... Most think white women look better," says another.

The bottom line is, we don't usually believe it's true love when we see black men with white women. Leslie in Atlanta said, "What first hits me is, 'Hmmm, gee... why?' Just simply 'Why?' It's hard for me to think, 'Well, gee, they're probably together because love is color blind and they truly care about each other.' I don't think that. Again I think, 'I wonder why he is with this white woman? What are the reasons?' Especially if she is not particularly attractive... I'm thinking, 'What is he doing with her?' "

After I finish going off in my head, I tell myself that I need to get a life. It's not my business that these two people are together. I have nothing to do with what goes on between them. But we view it as a rejection of black women. "Something just goes through me when I see it," said Tina. "In my mind, the black man is thinking the white woman is better. In reality she is not better. She's just white."

It's common for many to say that black men will go for the most unattractive white women, just as long as they are white. The truth is there are a lot of black men out there with beautiful white women. Black women are dealing with more than rejection by black men when they see these couples. We are upset with the black man, but also angry with the white woman.

As we grew up, everything outside of our households told us that white was beautiful. While our parents may have told us we were beautiful and laid a solid foundation, once you step outside you soon see that society's image of beauty does not reflect you. It reflects white females. "it has a subliminal impact when you look in the mirror," said Linda, who believes that on some level black women strive to meet society's definition of beauty. She added that we've come a long way. And you find more women going afrocentric these days. "Women in general are defined by society's definition... women are perming their hair, going to the gym, and if they don't see any improvements they have a low opinion of themselves. They feel they're deficient... Color adds to the problem... [Black women] don't come close to fitting society's image of beauty and there is no achievement because she is not white."

"It's difficult to be affirmed," said Rene, explaining how insecurities are compounded. "I still wonder if the brother finds the other more attractive than me. The attractive white girl or the light-skinned sister with the long hair... Then you must go to work and prove yourself, refute assumptions, rebut inferiority... and all you want is someone who says you are beautiful."

Black women, with exceptions, don't want to be white. We want to be valued, we want to be thought of as beautiful, too, inside and out. We see our beauty and our depth and it hurts and angers us when we are not viewed in that light by society. Naturally some of our resentment is going is to be directed toward white women who are looked upon more favorably. It is just intensified when we perceive that black men agree with society's image.

Greg does not believe black women's beauty is lost on black men. "In my opinion there is nothing more beautiful on this earth than a sister. We as a people are so beautiful. The shades, tones, colors, and personalities. The styles and looks are so varied. That's the beauty of it."

I think most black men share Greg's opinion and feel an allegiance to black women. However, almost all of the men interviewed have been involved with white women at some point in their lives. They said their attraction was based more upon the fulfillment of their needs than skin color, and added that white women believe they understand the black man's struggle. As a result, many black men are convinced white women understand them more than black women because they see the obstacles being set in place against them. When they come together, she puts as little pressure on him as possible.

Upon first hearing this comment, I asked in frustration how a white woman could "understand the dynamics of a racist society" more than a black woman? The response: "The difference is that the black woman is living in the racist society with the black man versus the white woman who is not subject to it. The black woman is upset and frantic whereas the white woman is on the outside looking in." But he adds, "Long term, this is no good because her way of being more easy-going isn't going to help him address the issues he must address. Black men need to understand growth of circumstance."

Following that interview I asked other men if white women are more sympathetic to their plight. All agreed. Greg said, "Many are trying to be more receptive... to understand the plight of the black man in America. I don't know if [they] are doing it for some self-gratification or if they are doing it for the betterment of the people. But it's refreshing to see someone who is sensitive to our needs."

"A white woman can relate to black men better than black women," said Lou. "They have heard the racist comments over the years from white men and they disagree with them...

"Educated white women realize that black men are climbing a steep hill. An educated black woman may appreciate that as well but an uneducated black woman will tell a man, 'Get your ass out of this house and come back with it...' "

Jenny, an educated black woman from Los Angeles, said she is not interested in any excuses a man may have for his inability to be a success in life. "Don't use the white man as a crutch... Get your ass up and go to school and do what you have to do!"

In response, Jenny's boyfriend Samson and his cousin Earl, who is from Atlanta, complained that black women just don't get it. They believe black women's attitude is, "'I've got mine, get yours,' and then women wonder why they're alone or having problems with their men."

"If you're going through a difficult time and [a white woman] is listening and caring, I can see how a brother could think, 'You know, this woman really understands me,' " said Earl.

"Which one would you choose," nodded Samson, "if one is feeling sorry for you and stroking you and the sister is saying, 'Nigger, get your ass up... Talking 'bout you some head of the household?!' "

In a falsetto voice, Earl chimed in, "'You ain't making no money!' "

"I dated a lot of black women," said Charles, whose fiancee is white. "And I became frustrated because their expectations were high... A lot of the women that I was attracted to and I was attracting were very materialistic. Not very genuine. They weren't looking for relationships. They were looking for step-ups just to better themselves.

"In my situation... I was looking to keep the race intact and stay within, and please my mother and father. ... I really found it was a matter of making myself happy and somebody accepting me for me. And this woman... does that for me. She just happens to be white. And I don't see that as a negative.

"Life is short and it's hard enough to find somebody to accept you for who you are and what you are. And if you can find someone who can do that, I don't think it's right to eliminate them because they don't have the right religion or skin color...

"I found someone who respects me for who I am, and loves me for who I am and what I am. I just can't see myself eighty-sixing her because she's not the right color."

Having said that, Charles believes white women can be more accepting of black men for who they are because they don't have as many self-esteem issues as black women. "My observation, is white women don't have as much baggage as black women because they weren't placed at the bottom of the totem pole by society."

On the flip side, the concept of black women with white men does not necessarily sit well with Charles. He has problems with it. And he had to learn to manage his frustration when many of the black women he knew became involved with white men following their break-ups with him. He attributes their gravitation to the materialistic nature of those women and the self-image problem black women battle.

The women he dated were from diverse professional backgrounds and Charles said they would not settle for a man earning a six-figure salary. "They wanted someone earning $1,000,000 per year, and that usually falls into the area of the white man... I'm not going to try to get inside their heads... maybe they were in denial about being black and they wanted to be white and they thought if they were with a white man, they would be more accepted by society."

There are other men who may not be happy when black women date white men, but who understand the choice may be a result of exhausted efforts in relationships with black men. Martin, 40, said he tries to give black women the benefit of the doubt and not assume they've given up on black men. It could mean a woman is colorblind or formed the relationship out of friendship. However, his subconscious says, "There goes another sister [who] can't find a good brother." His real fear is of the black woman's independence. He can imagine more and more black women remaining single and choosing male role models for their children, instead of seeking a partner for financial support.

Lou, a teacher, advises his male students to exclude uneducated black women. "If she doesn't have a job and a car, forget her because she'll break your back... She must at least have that. That usually means she has an education."

Women, on the other hand, don't have as many options. He said, "I understand the numbers problem... The majority of black women have no choice but to be open to a man without a job because they outnumber black men by such a great margin. Then you have to consider the black men who are married, in jail, or gay... Do you know how many lines of women there are outside the penitentiaries? You aren't going to find too many men with a job and a car!"

Greg can perceive that a black woman and white man are together based on love, but the image still bothers him. "He may truly love her. I don't know, looking at it from the outside. But it does set off a twang in me. I just think there are so many black men out there who would love to be appreciated by a black woman. It kills me a lot of times when I see a black woman with a white man because the first thing that comes to my mind is that we had 400 years of that—forced. White men forced themselves on our black women. And now that you have choices that you can make as to who you deal with... if the situation is entered into simply because this man is white, I've got a problem with that."

He feels just as angered by black men who date white women exclusively. "That says to me, you're saying there are no good qualities possessed by black women. So what does that say about your mother? Your grandmother? What does that say about any black females in your life? They don't warrant that type of love? There's nothing good about them? I've got a problem with that."

Many black women don't consider white men an attractive option simply because they have such a strong desire to raise a family with an African-American man. But like black men with white women, the women who are more open-minded often discover the fulfillment they are searching for—a sense of value.

"I have one sister who is married to a white man and another who is involved with one," said Raisa. "Both men take care of them in a manner that I don't think many black men would if they were able to. And I must say, I'm looking for any little thing to say, 'He's disrespecting you.' And it's not there."

Shayla married a black man but easily saw herself settling down with a white or European man because they seemed to be more attracted to her. "I didn't just wake up and say, 'I'm not going to date black men, I'm going to date white men.' Non-black men were the men who gave me the attention and they were the men I responded to."

White men, she said, are raised to take care of their families and be the breadwinners. Whereas, she adds, black men today don't want that responsibility and are looking for "... roommates, fifty-fifty. I don't understand because I didn't grow up like that.

"A white man said to me, 'Black women are so easy to please... all you want is someone to care for you... but you see, I was raised that way... You're not asking anything of me that I can't give to you, because that's what I'm supposed to do.'

"And that is the way I raise my son," she said of 12-year-old Tony. "I say, 'You are the man, you are the breadwinner. You love and take care of your wife.' "

Finola, whose London-born husband is black, said professional black women may turn to white men because they think, "Why be bothered with [black men's] arrogance? You want someone who will respect and value your existence... Maybe white men think you are more exotic and that is the attraction, but who cares if he thinks I'm special and he is treating me accordingly? White women haven't needed anything material from black men... 'Just give me some good loving.'"

Finola is the higher income earner in her household and she believes in the same vein as white women, "Black women are reaching that point with their financial success and entering into relationships with different perspectives. [We] are more accepting of a man who is just a good person, and black men are not. I find that offensive."

Rene said, "without apology," she could see herself marrying a white man. "I've dated a lot of black men and I've dated three white boys. Every white man who was a part of my life treated me like a princess. Every black man I've let into my life and seriously tried to love, treated me like a doormat...

"I dropped every one of those white men because I felt guilt. I felt shame every time I walked down the street because I [thought] I wasn't being loyal to my community." But now, she continued, "I know these boys know I'm a straight-up sister. I am firmly situated in the black community and the black tradition. They know it, understand it, and accept it. They love me just the same. So I know I can be myself. I can be committed to my community, as I am when I am with a black man.

"And not only that. I'm getting the love and support at home that I need to come out here and struggle everyday. So that's why I know I could marry one. Hell yes! I'm going home and get my butt kicked by a black man, when I can have a white boy who's going to kiss me? I just don't think so. If I go on a date with one, brothers look at me and roll their eyes. Roll them! Because my experience tells me that if I were out with you, you'd be dogging me right now... I have no guilt."

Despite Rene's pessimism, I could hear the continued hope for success in a relationship with a black man. She said, "It is because they're black and I'm black, And I want to have black children. I look at my brothers and they're good men. There are [other] black men in my life who are good people. I have a few girlfriends who are married or seriously involved and they have good men who are loving, supportive, faithful, and hardworking. And that helps me to keep the faith and believe that maybe if I'm patient and kiss enough frogs, there may be a prince."

"I also want faith because I want to keep our community together. At the risk of sounding arrogant, I think I'm a pretty on sister and I want to share myself and my accomplishments and all the fruits that they bring, financial and otherwise, with a brother.

"Also, in spite of a lot of the things I've said, I'm a Christian woman. I attend church every Sunday, a black church with black folks who are happy to be a part of the black tradition. And my religion teaches me to have faith and patience."

The essence of what black men and women want is the same: to be loved, understood, and respected for who they are. That desire transcends color and is felt by all people. The variable with black men and women is their added sensitivities in a society where they are prejudged on a daily basis.

There are women like myself who feel an anger that was born from what we internalize in society. This anger... this rage, can make it difficult to overcome our own prejudices. The irony may be that black men, who are the most downtrodden, are probably among the least prejudiced and racist people of all. The average black man is not out to get the white man in retaliation for all he has been put through. He simply wants a level playing field and his fair share of the pie.

A gentleman once asked me if I thought black men were more "macho" than other men. "Latin men," he said, speaking of his culture, "are more macho than white men." I told him my experience had been years of working around men much more than women, and also knowing black men of all types socially. I found all men to have extremely large egos, which I equate with machismo. It's just that some men are in a position to flex or exercise their machismo more than others due to money, power, or status.

Black men are macho or have large egos with an awareness of how a black woman is likely to respond to them and what she is likely to expect in return.

During the course of the interviews, men overwhelmingly felt that black women know what to do to please them and make them feel good, but refuse to be accommodating.

"Women aren't catering to men anymore," said Anthony. "They don't care about what makes him feel good. I think being attentive to a man makes him feel good."

"We all need stroking at some point in time," said Greg. "If she says, 'Well baby, you know you can only do what you can do. And you're doing the right thing...' Stroking like that can do wonders. Sometimes that's all it takes. Sometimes it takes a little less, sometimes a little more, but the need is there. And you need to be able to know that you can get that from the person in your life."

Women were cavalier if they acknowledged the importance of a man's ego. Often they were reluctant. Remember Sherry and the taxicab scenario? "I'm sensitive to it, to the extent that it doesn't take much out of me." And Tina feels that once she is in the relationship there should be no need to continue to let her man know he turns her on. "If I've got to keep working at it... it's not worth it."

Leo was among the men who believe black women are resentful towards black men because throughout history they have had to carry the heavy responsibility and weight of their family by themselves. "The essence of the family unit has always been primarily the responsibility of the black woman. So is she aware of the black man's ego? Quite frankly it has not been imbedded in her that the motherf—ker should even have an ego.

"The black woman is not going to subjugate herself to her man. She's not! But she'll subjugate herself to a white man because he is the essence of what being a man is about. Especially if he's successful and coming home and doing all that sh— she thinks she wants. But she is not going to do that for a black man.

"If she is married to a black man who has money and is providing for her financially, she is still going to think she can call the f—-g shots. You know why? Because he's a black man with money."

My expectations of black men are different from my expectations of white men, possibly to a fault, but not for the reasons black men have cited throughout this book. I expect black men to be sensitive, caring, and understanding of me as a human being, partner, and lover. A white man may be capable of these sensitivities towards me. However, with a few exceptions, it has not generally been my experience. My expectations regarding a white man's genuine consideration toward me are not high. And this may be attributed to my insecurities more than our actual interaction. I expect more from black men because they are aware of my existence as a woman who is black.

In reality, a black man's needs could outweigh the importance he will place on a black woman's burdens and her added sensitivities. And he then eliminates her without allowing an exploration of the possibilities of a fulfilling relationship.

Black men who "opt" for white women may hold black women to a different standard than other women by assuming black women will not fulfill their needs and that they will have different expectations than other women. Expectations beyond what some men believe they are capable of meeting or have a desire to meet. A black man, for example, may see a black woman's strength in overcoming her own obstacles as being in conflict with his needs and cast her aside.

So I dare say, it all boils down to the black man's ego.

Is a black woman who has received an education and succeeded in her profession more likely to be materialistic than a white woman who has been surrounded by wealth or advantages most of her life as suggested? An educated white woman may be aware of the steep hill the black man is climbing because she knows the side that is holding him back. But is she more likely than a black woman to help him continue the climb indefinitely?

In my view, no person with white skin can know the reality of the hurt and emotion felt when you are considered different, unequal, or simply less by society because of your color. Black men and women know the reality, and the truth, and the richness and depth of their beauty.

A white woman can be sensitive to a black man's plight because of her own obstacles. But hearing that she is considered more accepting of him than a black woman or has a greater awareness of his struggles is painful and I believe incorrect.

My sentiments notwithstanding, these beliefs, as held by some black men, should not be ignored. They reflect desires that are not being fulfilled. The man is obviously one of the two people in the relationship. As in the case of the woman, if his needs are never fulfilled, everyone loses.

As in many cases with women, a man may permanently place his sense of being and pride ahead of what he knows to be his woman's needs and sensitivities, and soon both are casualties of a relationship that crashed and burned. It can be an unnecessary and selfish weeding-out process. Instead of withholding, there could have been a giving, growing experience in which both parties won no matter what the outcome.

While I was mourning my relationship with Josh, a male friend couldn't believe the amount of time that had gone by without Josh reaching out to me. He said, "There are three things a man needs. You must have been lacking in one of these areas. No. 1, a man needs a woman who is going to give him space. No. 2, he needs someone who is going to believe in him. No. 3, she has got to be able to make good love to him."

I knew I had not been lacking in any of those areas. My sensitivities and needs have never been extreme. And yet they have always been difficult for men to fulfill. Their needs and my shortcomings seemed to always be in the forefront of their minds. This seemed to go along with their desire to view me on a lower level than themselves.

Josh particularly complained that he wanted me to show him more domesticity, especially to cook. He wanted to attribute my resistance to indifference and stubbornness. He would not fulfill my need to spend time together and have intimacy or my need for support and encouragement of my goals, which were necessary for me to want to cook for him. On the occasions that I cooked he immediately inquired about the next time. But he wasn't willing to put in the time together to raise my comfort level in the kitchen. Instead he wanted me to overcome my inexperience and anxieties and just do it randomly so he could see the desire.

Josh later said that he knew how much I loved him and believed in him. But love was not enough. An excellent chef in his own right, he said he had basic needs, such as a woman cooking for him, that I demonstrated I was unwilling to undertake.

Of course, cooking was not the actual problem but the importance Josh placed on it is an example of the lack of consideration he gave to my peace of mind and contentment. He had a complete awareness of me as a person and what I desired, but there was no concrete action on his part that attested to my needs as his priority or warranting his attention. It was not that he couldn't deal with my needs. He did not want to address them. He only wanted to address his own. He said himself that he knew what my needs were but he didn't know if he had a desire to fulfill them.

We all want to be loved. Even the unkind among us. If black men and women do not begin to express respect and sensitivity to each other's needs we may find we are among the last generation parented by African-American parents. Unfortunately this would be the result of African-American men and women giving up on each other, rather than transcendence of race.

9

THE MESSAGE IN THE MADNESS

What do you see when you look at young black kids today?

Kenny

I see an increased acceptance [of], tolerance [of], and participation in violence. This is displayed in their attitude and vocabulary, not just guns. Their self-esteem is skewed and based on a different nurturing experience than my own. For example, I excelled in school. Today self-esteem among youths hinges heavily on being tough and [having] a substantial income at a young age.

Shayla sees the lack of respect between young boys and girls.

There is no family structure, no guidelines. They're confused, wild, and bewildered.

Men aren't playing their active role in the house. They are trying to do it outside of the house with their girlfriend on the side and it's not working because kids are being affected. You can't run your household outside.

Kids are saying, 'Hey, if it's okay for Daddy to get up and go live with Suzie or whoever, then I guess it's okay.' Men have created those thoughts and feelings in children.

Cathy

... I fear they are being written off. They're looked at as, 'We can't do anything with them. We're just going to ignore them. Whatever happens, happens. We'll try to save ourselves, write this generation off and start with the next generation.

Mica

I feel they are the lost generation...

Peter

Their future looks grim... Parents are not taking care of business.

Group Interview

Earl

... It's lost. I hate to say it but we just need to look at the generation behind them.

Ed

Oh, don't say that! They are our future.

Jenny

... It is up to the parents. Sometimes you can have negative role models in your family and they can become positive role models if the child is taught those are people [he or she] doesn't want to be like.

Leslie

I say the same thing. The best thing you can do for your child is do something for yourself. Because they are going to emulate you in some shape, form or fashion somewhere down the road.

Charles

I think role models should be established in the home first. I think a kid's first heroes should be his mother and father. And Michael Jordan and Charles Barkley after that. Because if you're a parent and you allow Darryl Strawberry and Charles Barkley to be your kid's role models, you're putting your kid's life in the hands of somebody that you have no control over.

(Charles was interviewed separately.)

If Barkley and Strawberry f—- up. that's fine. But if the son's first role model is his father, then the father is in control and he doesn't have to totally depend on someone who is out of his control... Parents should be the first role model and everyone else is secondary. And then when these people fall from grace, kids still have their parents as role models.

Does it take a village to raise a child?

Erroll

I don't think my neighbors disciplined me, but I definitely had to give my neighbors respect... or I definitely knew they would tell my parents and I would get in trouble.

Now when someone tries to chastise a child... by just saying something to them, [the child] can go tell their parents [knowing] their parents are going to come and defend them.

Samson

That's the problem. Because I know if someone tries to tell me my kids did something, they did it as far as I'm concerned.

Earl

I've been cursed out... I told someone I saw that their daughter wasn't going to school.

She said, 'Well, you don't know what she was doing!' I said, 'Okay, forget it.' And it just so happened that this little girl who is 16 is now a mother herself. And that could've been prevented if the mother would have said, 'Where did you see her?'

Jenny

It goes back to respect. I mean whether she wanted to hear what you had to say or not, she owed you the respect to listen. Because what if one day she didn't go to school and she got snatched.. Now how is that child going to grow up to respect somebody when she sees her parents disrespecting people everyday?

Are black women raised with a low opinion of black men?

Kenny

Definitely. My mother-in-law tried to discourage my wife from becoming involved with me because I'm dark-skinned and [to her] that meant I was irresponsible.

Shayla

Single women may be.

Shayla was a single mother for 8 years. She and her son's father have always maintained a close supportive relationship.

But [I can understand how a woman who mothers a child with a man who] takes off and is not on the scene at anytime, might raise that child to see the father in a negative light.

You throw darts at the dad, you're going to hit the child.

Greg

Greg never knew his father. He and his mother grew together. She never tried to create negative images of men in his mind.

She always tried to make sure I understood what a good man is. And what a man should do. And just how a man should conduct himself.

He thinks his mother may be one of the exceptions.

[Other mothers] may relay their bad experiences to their daughters. She vents her pain and her daughter absorbs it. When she grows up, those things her mother told her in her formative years stay on her mind. She calls on them when it comes to dealing with a black man. She may have negative connotations in her mind before anything has happened. She's already thinking, he's probably shiftless, lazy, or irresponsible. That's what she has been bombarded with growing up. There are a lot of women who bring that baggage into the relationship.

You don't know a person until you get to know him. So what happened with your mother or your experiences may have absolutely nothing to do with the person you are trying to deal with or the person who is trying to deal with you.

Rene

... I grew up in a house with a stepfather who worked every day and brought home a paycheck, but he was an alcoholic and very physically abusive to both me and my mother. As result I think I never pictured myself raising a child with a man. I always pictured myself as a single parent. And I've always been out here feeling like I can and will do this by myself, simply because my perception of what it's like to live with a black man was shaped by my stepfather. My position is, if that's what it means to have a black man in my life, I don't want it. I mean I'll never be financially dependent upon one. Because they will kick your butt for the favor of giving you a little financial assistance...

So to the extent that statistics suggest that many of us grow up in single female-headed households, [which] shape our perceptions of black men and what they can be counted on to do for us; in many instances that's absolutely nothing, or the other extreme, which is something very bad...

Sherry

If I could only have one child... I'd rather have a daughter in this society. Because she is more likely to come through and skate. Now I don't know who she is going to marry. But there's a whole lot more... distractions...out there for sons. And I hope to have a son one day. But there [is] lots of negativity.

... The pressures are greater on men... 'I'll go out and make some money for Mama today.' I don't think girls feel that. They might feel like, 'I want to help out,' but they don't feel like, 'I need to do this because there is no man in the house. I'm the man.'

Boys are more likely to get caught up in those negative things, be it drugs or whatever, or feel frustrated because they can't accomplish what they want to.

10

The Varying Images
of Black Men

Is the black man's stock high?

Leo

Not on a broad spectrum. Educated black men, yes. Their stock is very high. Their sh— is at a premium. And then you go further, an educated black man who's making money. Let's take it like this, one percent of the population makes $100,000. So you tell me is their stock high? Yeah, the numbers tell me their stock is high. For the most part there are more black males in jail than there are in college.

Do you think it's interesting that black men's stock is high on one hand and on the other hand they are considered by some as the lowest on the totem pole?

Sherry

I believe, and a lot of black women don't, that for the most part it is harder for a black man to achieve in this world than it is for a black woman.

I think both race and gender are factors in just about everything in society, It certainly is a factor in employment and advancement. In many positions, certainly at entry level, it is much easier for a woman to walk in and get a job than it is for a black man with the same qualifications and background. That's because society sees her as less of a threat... A woman is much more likely to be in a better position financially or otherwise because society is willing to give her the opportunity.

Is it saying anything that a woman's stock is higher in society and lower in the relationship? It's always a struggle for black people in a relationship because race always seems to creep in on any given day. And it's going to affect how you interact with each other.

I imagine a black man may feel, 'I went to work today and this is what happened... society told me in so many ways... A cab passed... I went to wherever and they thought I was the messenger...' When he goes home to his household, how does that make him react? Does that make him act like it's important to be dominant in that sphere? I don't know?

Are you sensitive to that type of thing with your husband?

Sherry

Probably not as much as I should be.

I guess the next statement I'd like to make is that I don't think my husband and I have that problem. But I'm sure we do. Now that I think about it, may be that's why he acts the way he does sometimes... because it's very important for him to have a realm of the world, where he can feel like he has some authority or control.

And I say that without saying that I live with a very authoritative or dictatorial man. I do think maybe that encourages black men to act the way they do. To explore options where they have options, because they have so few options.

Frustrations

Leo

You know one of the things I find myself striving for? Objectivity. That's something I really try to force myself to do. I always look at something from the other side.

That's probably why I'm so quick to argue the point when people just blatantly say that I don't understand something simply because I have a difference of opinion. Which quite frankly, as a black man, I find myself constantly having to prove... that I understand! Why do I have to prove I understand? Assuming I'm a rational, intelligent individual, why isn't everyone else held f——g accountable as to whether they understand or not?

That's just part of being a black man. It might seem minute, but you'd be surprised at how many times during the course of a day that you have to deal with that... 'Prove you understand, motherf——ker.' I'm tired of it!"

Lou

Everywhere in America and the world, black men are stereotyped as violent, athletic, funny, not-so-smart people... and that's what hurts me the most...

Contentment

Leo vs. his father-in-law

You know what's interesting? [My mother-in-law] is a strong black woman. [She] is educated. [My father-in-law] isn't, which is so typical of so many couples of their generation. For years he has listened to his wife's sh—. she has run her mouth and given him more sh— than you can shake a stick at. And now he's 70 plus, retired with heart problems, and he's finally standing up after all these years and essentially saying to his wife, 'No. f— you,' in his way.

I'm not going to wait until that time. I'm starting the sh— off the way it is going to be. I don't f— with you. You don't f— with me. If we can get along, fine. I am very confident in my ability to find someone who will fit into my role in terms of what I need... I don't give anybody any sh—. But you know what I'm even more adamant about? I ain't taking an iota of sh— either.

Lou

A black woman will send a guy running. He's not ducking his responsibility as he will be labeled. He's searching for happiness. Whereas if she leaves, her search for happiness is understood.

11

"I Find Myself Being Just That Way"

Samson

Greg

Some women are more concerned with how you look and what you drive and how you dress as opposed to what type of person you are. So many women get caught up with what is on the outside and don't really care what is on the inside...

Men are more receptive to an average-looking woman who is just going to love them and care for them. Not one who makes X amount of dollars. Just a woman who loves him for him. He's more inclined to accept her. A woman may not give the man she might be inclined to look at the same consideration if he doesn't make the right amount of money.

... Many [women] will be quick to tell you, 'If he's not doing as well as I am, then he warrants no consideration.' They aren't even doing that well themselves. But they figure whatever plateau they're on, the man they deal with should at least be on the same level, preferably on a higher level...

Anthony

I've met women who are looking for a man who is going to take care of them. He might be the worse person or the worse lover, but she doesn't care.

Are concerns that black men no longer consider black women beautiful, valid?

Group Interview

Erroll doesn't think black women are completely wrong when they say black men no longer recognize their beauty because so often black men are attracted to black women who have the physical characteristics that are closer to white women. "Good hair" light complexion, et cetera.

Erroll

If a black woman gets a natural, black men will dog her out. 'Why'd you cut your hair?' I hear that all the time...

A girl cut her hair at work, all the black men were commenting negatively about her hair.

So what is that saying? That's saying that she is doing something that she feels is good for her. She feels good about it. They don't see it as that. They're not attracted to it. So what's attractive to them? Long hair, soft hair. What's soft hair, what's light skin? The things we associate with beauty are closer to white.

Earl

And then [women] internalize it. Because who were the hard little rough girls at school? The darker-skinned girls. Because none of the guys were telling them they were pretty. It was always the lighter-skinned girls. The red bones. They got all the attention and had some sway to their walk.

Darker-skinned girls said, 'Who you looking at!' Because they internalized that vibe we hit. We didn't have to say, 'You're ugly,' but everything we did said the darker you were the uglier you were.

The light/dark problem is another part of the baggage we carry with us. Erroll said darker-skinned sisters are often told, 'You're pretty to be dark.' He thinks those who make such statements don't realize the depths of what they have internalized from white society.

Samson

I find myself being just that way. But you know what? You have to fight through that everyday... because it will get you and you cannot let that overwhelm you.

Sometimes I see white girls look at me and I just keep on going. I don't give them no respect.

Earl

Yeah. You have to wake up and check yourself every morning.

The Taboo

Dennis

Society says blacks should only be with blacks... It's not to say, 'I'm a black man, I'm macho, and I can have a white woman.' It's just to say, 'You say I can't have a white woman or a white wife, and I do.'

... Or 'Society says this is not right and it is... It's right between her and I and she's white and I'm black... It feels right and society says it shouldn't and it does.'

Although I admit, in most cases black men go out with white women just to say, 'I've had a white woman.' Because they know they can get a black woman. That's not a lay-up. A black woman is a lay-up.

It's a little easier to establish a relationship with a black woman than a white woman. That's because we share a history... On the other hand, the history of black men and white women is very limited and sometimes that serves as the attraction.

Martin

The attraction [to white women] was something taught... A forbidden fruit desire.

There is also the stereotype of the black male as being more potent and durable... When the two forces come together, men just to want try it.

... The mentality is I can have a sister whenever I want her. But not the white woman. I better take this opportunity.

... There is no difference between the two sexually. Except, sisters are more mental and men fall short and can't deal.

12

Black Women –
Life Experiences vs.
Opportunities vs.
Choices

Sherry

I wonder if black women are the social economic climbers that white women are...

I can sincerely tell you, I really didn't think I'd ever get married. I was the high school kid who didn't have a lot of dates. I thought there were more attractive women than me out there. The guys I was interested in were interested in other people. So any ambitions I had did not involve a man. If I met a man, great. But if I wanted nice clothes, a nice home, whatever, I felt it was all on me.

And so my priority was going to school and getting an education. Trying to become whatever it was I wanted to become, so I wouldn't have to worry about a man who was going to help in this endeavor.

And to the extent that I did [meet a man] it was a welcome surprise.

... I think many women feel that way. They may be unaware of it. It may be evidenced in the way they channel their energy. Their ambitions are for themselves instead of through a man...

The point is there are plenty of secretaries out there who are looking for a man, black or white, who is going to help them move up the ladder. That is their perception of how to get ahead... In my personal opinion and experience, it is more likely to be a white woman who thinks this way than a black woman. Now that may be because society has told us black men will not be permitted to pull you up, so you may as well do it yourself.

Maybe the black secretaries don't look at the black attorneys with the same smacking of the chops as the white girls I remember. The girls from college were all over the ball players [saying], 'Well sh--, if he makes it to the NBA, we're set.'

It may be a total percentage issue. For instance, here's a scenario: if 20 to 25 percent of black or white women are likely to look for a man, the fact is black women are only 12 percent of that. There will be fewer who are out there doing what it takes to get a man who is looking for a woman. So you put them in the workforce where may be 15 percent of the secretaries or paralegals are black. Of the black and white attorneys, maybe 20 are always looking out. Plenty of attorneys are married to for-

119

mer paralegals or secretaries. And many women are not discriminating as to whether he is black or white. The point is, 'Who is going to better my condition?' And there are ten times as many [white women]... The odds are they are going to get more of them.

... There are also plenty of black women who don't want to be with black lawyers [or professionals] because they feel their experiences are so different... You have to understand, if you're someone who has grown up in the heart of Brooklyn, for example, and you're a secretary here [in Manhattan], and you just love Brooklyn... the drug dealers are not knocking at your door. You're fine and your family is fine. You've got black people all around you. You come in here everyday and do your nine to five. You don't necessarily want to get with a man who is going to have you living on the Upper West Side of Manhattan, where you're lucky to pass a black person every ten blocks.

Do you think black women really allow themselves that many choices?

She may be turned on to what the man is offering her. She may be turned off. I think it's totally personal. But I don't doubt some of them would be turned off. The social setting you take some people away from and place them in is too foreign in their eyes...

You know a man is not the be-all and end-all for everybody. If my man told me he was going to live in the North Pole... I don't think I'd move to the North Pole for a man.

Are some black women coming to a realization within themselves that marriage and family may not be attainable?

Leo

Sure. Let me ask you a question. Have you interviewed any black gynecologists? Because they see it from a whole different perspective. I have friends who are

120

gynecologists who tell me they have patients who are attractive professional black women, mid to late thirties and over. They come in and say 'F—- it, I'm having my tubes tied. I'm not having any babies. I don't want any babies.' And they have the operation and six months, a year and a half later, they come back after finding the man of their dreams, 'Got to untie them, Doc.' Interview a gynecologist, they see all the sh—. You're going to see the vacillation is there in terms of black women. They don't know what they want.

(Following Leo's interview a gynecologist confirmed that in his experience there have been a great number of black women who have had such a procedure reversed after meeting 'the man of their dreams.')

Leo

Don't get me wrong. I'm not saying this only exists in black women, but that's who we're talking about. They've gone from having an unwillingness to give h—d, to where some of them realize, 'There's nothing wrong with giving h—d. And you know what? I kind of like it.' I've seen that in my lifetime. I've seen that maturation. And you know what? [Other women] have always given h—d. They would rather give it. And it's not a big thing with them.

Black women are just discovering themselves. Let's face it, how old is Essence magazine? Ten, twenty years ago women didn't have the black hair magazines they now have. Black women, they're new on the scene to themselves!

Rene

I think some sisters decide that being a mother and a wife isn't the be-all and end-all. They want to be career women. They want to be Oprah. They want to be out there making money. Marriage, family, and the house with the white picket fence is simply not a lifestyle that appeals to them. I think living in the post-women's rights revolution has made women realize that it's okay to make that decision. And women are making it. I think that's true of many women.

It's also true that some women are resigning them-selves to what they believe they can have. And maybe they don't believe they can have the white picket fence, the man, and the children. So they're readjusting their goals and expectations.

For me, I feel that's not the most important thing in this life. I want a companion. I want a man in my life... and right now I have a couple in my life... But I'm not so certain the children and the wife thing appeals to me that much. I've always felt that it does. But one of the men in my life is divorced with two children who he sees on the weekends. Usually I feel like I never want to do this. Then again, if they're my own...

I also feel the power to give life is such an amazing thing, I don't want to live and die without experiencing it... So I'm kind of conflicted. I want it all. I know my child would be a priority in my life, over work, etc... But I also know that if I never get married, I wouldn't feel my life was a failure.

Women and the workplace

Phillip

There are limited places within an organization where blacks can go. Different personalities are more acceptable than others, You can look at certain people and know if they'll go forward or not. Assimilation is extremely important.

... White men like a certain type of black woman. Only a certain type succeeds.

... Black women lag behind white women and black men because they have not always professionally posi-tioned themselves for advancement. [Black women] are shelf-sitters.

... Her traditional role is defined as being compla-cent and liking stability and security. She is quick to go after financial stability and then become complacent. But some go all the way... Although they are in conflict because [they are] competing with the black man... And then they have a whole new set of criteria that govern their life. And men still approach them in the traditional way And she is saying she doesn't need him.

Peter

White women come across more pleasant and less fearful than black women. Black women are more reserved and less open. [But] you can't be too open.

White women can appeal to a man's feeling of not [being] accepted by white society and then he lets his guard down. He'll say to himself, 'What's so wrong about this?'

At my company there are many black and white women. White women are more pleasant and the black women just look at you. The perception of acceptance is there [among white women] and you naturally gravitate towards what makes you feel comfortable.

If a sister is more friendly and open, a man is going to perceive it differently than if she were a white woman. He'll take it as the sister is 'interested.'

Why?

He would feel the white woman is only accepting him as a person vs. the black woman is looking for a relationship or something. She has ulterior motives.

Doesn't that demonstrate he is not giving her a chance?

True, he won't give her an opportunity to be a woman vs. a black woman.

It is just in our DNA that we feel we know where she is coming from, [her agenda]. ...What you are exposed to culturally, growing up, manifests itself [later].

13

Marriage and Relationships

Are you ready for marriage?

Greg

Emotionally, yes. I don't think my career is where I would like it to be... I don't think I'm ready to maintain the lifestyle I would like for us to have. She may come in here and say, 'Well, this is fine.' No, it's not fine. I would want to make sure, if nothing else, if she didn't want to work another day in her life, we would be able to maintain a style of living that I'd enjoy and hopefully she would enjoy also.

Cathy

I can't say [marriage] is a priority. I'm just trying to get comfortable with the idea... I'm not sure what it is... I guess in my parents' relationship, my father is very domineering...

He and my mother own a business. My mother has been to college, my father has not. In fact he never graduated from high school. And I think it makes him more comfortable that they own this business together. He's really the one that's pretty much in charge. My mother does all of the accounting and administrative work, but he's the one out there doing all the selling and talking on the phone.

... My mother has definitely made sacrifices in her life to do what [my father] thought was best. And I guess I've always been afraid of ending up in a relationship like that.

Have you ever withheld sex to get what you want?

Samantha

No. I've given sex as a way of making up. Withholding anything is negative.

127

Cathy

I've never done it to get something material. I think I've definitely done it to punish him because he did something I wish he hadn't done. Or he disagreed with something I thought was important.

Mica

Not consciously. But when I was not happy with his actions, I may not have wanted to and that could have been perceived as such.

Martin

My wife has done that. It can have detrimental affects. I take away her power by showing nonchalance.

Can it destroy trust?

Martin

No. But it can lead to straying. There is an underlying thought that in marriage the sex is always there... When she breaks that I might say, 'Sh—, if I can't get it from her, then I don't need to be here.'

Dion on sex

If I have something on my mind and you think that me having sex is going to ease my mind... Then you're wrong. That's not what I need. I need someone to talk to and share whatever is on my mind. Sex is only temporary.

Leo on sex

My wife has never used sex as a weapon. But I'll tell you how I feel it could be detrimental. I, as a man, would not accept my wife using sex to get what she wants...

This is an interesting statement I'm about to make. As a man I don't want to feel there is any p—y out ther so good that I can be held hostage by it. But being a intelligent man, I do realize there is p——y out there that is just that good, that... could hold me hostage. Because there's too many MFs that have much more going for them than I do, who have been held hostage by [sex with a certain woman] and have paid for it.

You see, it's like snorting cocaine. The fool thinks, yes, you can snort cocaine, but the fool who thinks he can get out there and snort all the cocaine and not have to deal with the downside is truly a fool.

The man who thinks that he's such a man that he can't get roped by any woman out there, well, he's truly a fool, too. 'Cause wars have been fought over that. I'm not foolish enough to think that couldn't happen to me.

Is it against a man's nature to be monogamous?

Charles

I think it's against men and women's natures. I think being monogamous is a learned thing.

How many men did you check out today? It's just like communicating. It's learned. It's not something you take for granted.

Greg

I don't think so. I think we all want variety. You can definitely have variety with the same person. When it comes to sex specifically, you can make sex an interesting thing. It doesn't have to be regimented. It doesn't have to be the same way, in the same place, on the same day. You can spice it up enough where it's new and different. And I think that's what people really crave. I don't think it's that we necessarily want different people. It's just that we want something different.

I think that if my woman knows that variety is something that needs to be maintained in a relationship and she is actively doing something to keep that newness and freshness there, I think that in itself can be satisfying.

I'm all for doing the same for her.

129

Peter

If you're together you should be committed to each other. If you are capable of fulfilling his needs and you know what they are, then he shouldn't stray. Men need ego stroking and will try to find that elsewhere.

If you discovered your mate was having a sexual relationship with someone else, would your reaction depend on the state of your relationship at the time?

Samantha

Unless we were separated, nothing would justify it. Monogamy is essential to my marriage. There is no other option.

Cathy

He would just die! And I tell him that. Every once in a while, I tell him, 'I'm just telling you, so don't act surprised.'

It's hard for me to think of any situation that I could get past. Even though in reality we've been together for so long, maybe we could. Maybe there is some situation where I wouldn't want to give up the whole relationship. But just thinking of it in the abstract, I don't think it could survive. But, never say never.

Hopefully it will never happen and I'll never have to make that choice.

Mica

Yes. I feel men straying is a part of any long-term relationship.

But regardless, it would be difficult to work through and I would never let him know that I would stay.

Linda

It is a major trust violation. It is going to hurt regardless of the circumstances. I will feel betrayed. And I'll feel bad for her as well, because she was deceived and disrespected too. He gave her the impression he was free and clear and he wasn't, if he was with me... So there is more than one victim.

Rene

There was a time when I felt [it depends on the circumstances]. Now I feel that behavior undermines trust. If he tells me he's monogamous and I find he's not, I have to leave.

Charles

In the past I would have always said no ['I could not forgive my wife,']. But yes, I think with just cause... I'd like to think I'm a bit more mature and a little bit more responsible than I used to be. You've got to be responsible for your actions. And a lot of times, men will drive women to be unfaithful. And vice versa.

I mean, if she's just a whore and f——g around for the sake of f——g around, that's one thing. If I can take a moral inventory of myself, and she told me this is the reason why.... and if I had caused it to happen, yeah, I could forgive her... [but] I'd never tell her that.

Greg

It would depend on the circumstances as far as whether or not I would continue to deal with her. If I was doing everything necessary in the relationship and she decided to stray, then I probably wouldn't deal with her.

If I was negligent in some areas, I'd also have a problem if she didn't express her concerns. But if we tried to talk about it and I still wasn't doing what I should have been doing, then I really couldn't blame her. She's human. She has needs. I'd look at it as my fault. Especially if she wasn't receiving the love she needed to receive.

131

Dion

Yeah, I could forgive her. I'd have to find out the reason. Could have been I drove her away. The thing is, she made the decision to do it. I didn't make her do it.

Sometimes you can be frustrated in a relationship and [if] you can't talk to the other person... someone [else] is going to comfort you... [either] sexually or by just talking...

Phillip

I could not forgive her. I don't need that type of relationship.

Kenny

It is a major trust violation... [But] it depends on the circumstances.

When I was in high school I had an experience that laid the foundation for my inability to trust. I discovered my girlfriend was dating someone else and I was literally on the verge of killing them both when a New York Post headline— 'Jealous lover kills them both'— flashed through my mind. At that moment, I turned and walked away.

I grew more from that instance, that night, than any other in my life. That's why I reiterate, never trust to the point where you lose or suffer if that trust is violated.

Martin on a man's infidelity

A man straying is not a reflection on her. It's true men inevitably mess around... Any woman who may want a particular married man, if the situation is right... she'll have him. Curiosity results in desire, which results in the challenge, which results in the conquest.

I would never leave home, but it doesn't mean I would not be intimate with another woman... There must be something I feel that draws me to her. The fact that she's fine is just part of the requirement. It's not a question of what they don't have... but even if it was gold, I wouldn't leave home. I'm bound and tied to my wife by responsibility as well as by choice...

What if you discovered she slept with someone else?

Martin

I wouldn't forgive her... Maybe over time, but chauvinism says that's mine and she shouldn't be giving it away.

My ego would be more hurt than anything. My relationship with my wife cannot be penetrated.

14

Spirituality

14

Spirituality

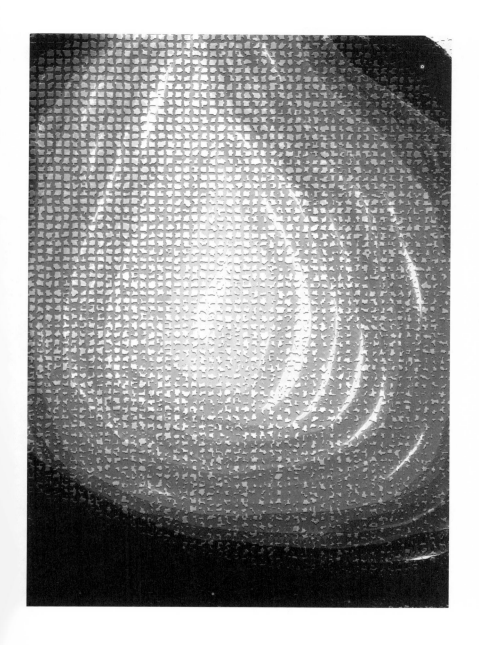

How important is the Spirit of God?

Phillip

[Spirituality] is not important. Some people are more earth grounded. Each person is different.

What do you rely on or draw from during difficult times?

Phillip

My strengths.

Regarding Spirituality

Leo

I think we come from a group of people who have historically been spiritually grounded. I don't think this generation of black men... is so far removed from their roots or their culture that they don't realize the spiritual pull. Now whether they heed it or not is different. But they certainly have to be cognizant of it.

Earl

... With the way the brothers are being pushed out of jobs, it's like they don't have anything else to fall back on... they're lashing out at people around them. He feels betrayed by the world. I'm speaking from personal experience. He feels betrayed by everybody, everything, every system that he ever trusted.

For years we were told, 'Go to school, get an education, college, and you'll be promised a good life.' Well, it didn't work. So now he has been betrayed by everything that's been drilled into him since he left his house to go into the first grade. You're lashing, and if you don't have God in your life and your woman does, you are unevenly yoked. It's going to be torture...because you feel betrayed and you don't have anything else.

Dion

When I date a person the number one thing it all starts with is does that person have a spiritual foundation. Because then you know what you're working with. You're not working with someone who is unsure of themselves versus someone who... has a strong spiritual background and a strong self-image. They let things outside get to them versus someone who is spiritually inclined.

Linda

God is my partner. I would be dead if he was not with me and I did not feel the inclinations and vibes that he has sent to me. I don't think there would be reason to continue living if God were not in my life... he keeps me up with Jesus Christ.

If I thought of my fate and plight in earthly terms, I'd be doomed. I believe I am worthy because of my faith in him. I am at his mercy. I believe in his opinion of me.

Tina

God plays a great role in my life. From the bottom to the top. If it wasn't for God, I wouldn't be here.

You know what? If I want anything, I pray to God and If I don't get an answer from God, I normally don't do it. That's how great a role he plays in my life.

... Black women are more [generally] spiritual.

... I like a church going man... Christian... Got to call on the Lord sometime.

Most of the time, if I find out he's not going to church, I won't date him. And I have to interview him in the beginning. I talk about the Lord a lot when I first meet somebody to see how they respond. If they don't respond and don't say anything about the Lord, then he's not spiritual enough for me.

Finola

A [solid] spiritual foundation is the only way it can work because of the burdens and struggles. You need a reason to make the relationship work.

My husband is not a Christian, but I believe in God and I believe my kids should be raised in the church... My concern is for my kids' souls.

Is spirituality something that is central in your marriage or in your life?

Sherry

I guess individually, but not as a group. I think we probably would be stronger if we were as a couple... I think I tend to be more religious and he tends to be more spiritual. Meaning that I have more rituals. I go to church, etcetera. But I think he is the deeper thinker about spirituality and what it means... I probably need to be a deeper thinker... Yes, there is some foundation there for both of us.

I always thought it would be good to marry a Christian because he would be accountable to someone other than me. I shouldn't have to worry about him being unfaithful because there is something more than just love that's saying you shouldn't be going out and doing this, that, and the other. Maybe that's not thinking enough of myself or the love bond, but I always thought that would make it stronger.

And so I do have a husband who I think is spiritual. He has a strong sense of right and wrong. But he's not religious in the sense that he believes the Bible is a book to be literally followed with the commandments, etcetera.

He is a Christian?

Sherry

... I don't know what to say to that. I mean, I think, yes. Has he looked it up and thought about this that and the other? Yes. Does he go to church Sunday or most Sundays? No, he doesn't.

I think his spirituality is based more on a God force than Christianity. And so to the extent that he is faithful, it doesn't have so much to do with a book of rules, but more his strong sense of right and wrong and what he wants for his own life.

141

15

Reflections of Men

The role of the man in the relationship

Peter

To be an equal partner. To be the sole provider financially. But some women want more involvement... To step up and be a true loving man. Understanding, sensitive, show hurt, solicit input. Respect his companion, which does not mean being controlling. Peacekeeper.

Irresponsible men

Peter

Some men are irresponsible. It ties into self-esteem. A man needs to be a man and feel like a man across the board... employment, women, education, or else he is selfish and closed in his views.

All brothers are not irresponsible.

On black women

Kenny

Within the larger American sexist society, she is seen as a nurturer. And it is quietly acknowledged that the woman is smarter. But to nurture something effectively there must be a root to take hold of... The black man has been uprooted so [the black woman] is ineffective in her classic role. She is extremely effective in her principal role of responsible individual. She is overcompensating. She understands what is lacking and she's doing a helluva job... But there is a conflict in the belief of the need to nurture the man...

Her role is to be supportive. To critique his ideas and perspectives. She has a historical perspective of him vs. white society's perspective...

Martin

The black man cannot meet the mental challenge of the black woman. Her role has gone from homemaker to the backbone of the family... Maybe she was always the backbone, she can and has led a family without a man, which has resulted in an abundance of successful men brought up by single mothers.

How socio-economic factors come in, I don't know, but her role has resulted in the diminishing role of the man as the power person, internally and externally. He is least respected and perceived as irresponsible with his family. At times he exploits his women or he allows himself to be exploited.

A stronger woman may not want to be alone and may make a worthwhile effort at a relationship while settling for less. They might bond and she may conform to the traditional role. But usually she puts more into it and he becomes irresponsible or she outgrows him.

Peter

Black women are always looking at the next level. There may be a really good black man she perceives to be at a lower level...

... In New York, the perception would be the more successful you are, the more of a man you are. That is a lie.

Leo

My friends are running women [having multiple sexual partners], spending money and doing the sisters wrong...

Peter

A real man wants to work with a woman. There should be an understanding that she must work with him as much as he must work with her. My issue is some women want things automatic.

Black Men in American Society

Kenny

The real problem is he has yet to define himself within society, and until he can with regards to education, employment, et cetera, he cannot relate to her. He needs a functional sense of self. His ability to get a job and

146

support himself and others must manifest itself before real progress can be made in the relationship.

Peter

I agree to a great extent that black women are not being raised to be supportive of a successful black man whereas white women are supportive... White women may be more so as a result of their upbringing and their passivity... The male brings home the bacon in the white environment.

The Male Ego

Peter

I don't think women have made it a point to practice supporting the male ego.

Dion

The male ego is very fragile... It's like a piece of glass... That's what he stands on... His ego can be torn down very easily. And even though some men may say they don't... that ego is there. If you take the ego out of the man, you take the man. He's no good.

He needs to know that he's doing the right thing. Or he needs to be met in the middle... where he's told, 'Well, honey, thank you for cutting the grass today.' Or 'Thank you for washing my car today.' ... Something like that. A man's needs are simple.

Anthony

Nothing secures a man or builds up a man more than knowing he has the right woman loving him and watching his back... knowing he has someone who is concerned about his needs.

You'd be surprised what the slightest touch does for a person. It's not good to be around someone who says he cares for you and you can count the times she's touched you in the past week. Or you always have to ask for something, she's never extending herself. You might go to hug her and she's not receptive...

147

Ed

Women are driven by love. Men are driven by ego.

Earl

I agree. I think women are driven by love because women love men more for what is on the inside. Men like women more for what is on the outside. And that has to say a lot.

Kenny

You must realize with men [and commitment] a lot has to do with timing, availability, access... You always think you can do better. So why settle?

This was a major factor for me until marriage.

It can prevent you from committing. The ego factors in. The ego bolsters, but it can also be deadly.

Responses to the 1972 Essence article 'The Black Woman'

Leo

I wholeheartedly endorse it...

I've just come to the first part I disagree with... the last sentence in the second paragraph, 'The black woman actually wants to see the black man take his place.'

Well, I'm from Missouri... I wouldn't have been as optimistic. Otherwise, I could see myself writing something exactly like it.

Dennis

The article describes the woman's roles as supportive and understanding, not demeaning in allowing the man to develop and take his place. In doing so she shares that place with him... A supportive woman keeps that foundation from shifting in the relationship.

... This suggests to me to not take her support for granted... not to diminish the values she brings to the relationship solely because she is supporting his decisions. It also suggests that he must fulfill her needs or she won't exist [she'll leave] and he won't have the support he desires.

Kenny

Great article. It is the solution to the problem. Union of one. Each party needs to understand.

Dion

I think that's basically it. It describes how a black man should be to his woman. He should be able to provide for her. Take care of home. But also share responsibilities.

I don't want to marry a woman so she can cook for me... clean for me... do my laundry. Because that's not what I'm marrying her for. See, I can already do those things. So I can just as well share those things. Because when you start to have children, the responsibility is not just on the woman. It's on the man too.

It's not like back in the 1950s or '60s... when he takes the obligation at the altar... to take care of that woman, that's what he's supposed to do. No matter what it takes.

She wants to feel at peace... secure. She wants to know that she doesn't have to worry. When a woman doesn't have to worry about her man... she's at peace. She's taken care of.

Charles

As a woman, I would be insulted by that. As man, I am not attracted to it... It does sound like something from 1972... I guess a '90s man has got to understand the point of view of a '90s woman.

I'm sure there's a lot of men who would be attracted to that.

I interpret it as a sort of a very docile, subservient woman... the man part was fine. If that's what a woman wants to do, that's fine. But that should not be the general role of the woman, in order for the relationship to work, that's what she has to succumb to.

I think it's ridiculous.

16

From Her Lips

Shayla

I think there have always been problems between black men and women. It was just more covered up in the past because women were not as verbal about it. They weren't boisterous. You know, like my mother, your mother, their mothers... It was just hush, hush, hush... something women just didn't talk about it.

My dad took care of our family financially, but I'm sure there were a lot of things that my mom needed... She needed a best friend. I believe he [should have been] her best friend...

Somehow, I think it's hard for women to forgive and forget.

Nowadays women like myself have jobs and bring home the bacon. They feel like they have freedom of speech.

In the Bible it says, 'we were to suffer through our labor and the man through the sweat of his brow...' Well, now the woman is doing both. She's given labor and she's sweating because she has to work.

I think women are just frustrated with that. She's saying if I have to have the kid... go out and work, and bring home the bacon, of course I'm going to have a lot to say. And I think there's a lot of anger there.

My brother has a beautiful little girl. He wanted a child for so long. He could never have a child. Now he has a child and a beautiful woman, inwardly and outwardly, and they are no longer together. Okay, that's fine.

But he goes out and moves in with somebody else and now the mother of his child is pregnant again by him. Now she's about to have a second child while he's living with someone else. I'm saying, 'Honey, now this is where you have to be responsible. It's not about your thrill. It's not about your pleasure. It's about you being responsible.'

A lot of men are just not responsible. I don't think they comprehend that word.

Men

Men have no fear. A man with no morals will do anything. I don't trust a man with no morals. You've got to fear a higher power. If you fear God then I know there are a lot of things you just won't do. But without that fear you're capable of doing anything and everything. Men nowadays are so heartless, unconcerned, uncaring. And you wonder, 'How did you get that way?

I think [many men] are narcissistic, because selfish people are out for their own pleasure. Once satisfied they're looking for higher highs and deeper depths. A man will say, 'I don't need one woman, but three women to satisfy me. Now I don't need just three women, but I need a man, a woman and something else.'

The more you expose yourself the more you're going to need to satisfy that urge.

Shayla's husband and love

Love is about commitment... wanting to share yourself with someone. Wanting to open up and allow someone to know you...

Love is not based on feeling... emotions change every day... It's based on commitment on trust.

I trust Lance with the things I say to him. Whatever I say to him, I know is going to stay with him. We try to sit down and understand each other and listen.

After a long frustrating day, I want to come home to someone who's going to comfort me and console me... as well as on a good day.

The man must be the provider, but the bottom line is caring for me.

Tina, 44, Atlanta

Black men, white women

I feel most black men can be a man to some other race, but not the black woman. They want to treat the black woman like she doesn't have power, and she's not a queen. But they'll treat another race like a queen. That's the part I don't understand.

I've heard white women say that black men treat them better than they treat black women. Even white women wonder why that is. I'd like to know why.

Do you ever think white women put forth a concentrated effort to take black men?

Some do. I think some do to aggravate black women because they know how black women feel about that... I know they do. They tell me they do it on purpose. And when they see a black woman coming towards them, if they are with a black man, they always go out of their way to hug or kiss him. When I see them coming I know what she's going to do. So I turn my head and I can almost see out the side of my eye that she's looking back to see if I'm looking. It's like she has to let you know that she's with a black man. That's the part that makes me mad.

I have white friends who are with black guys and I'm not mad with them. It's when they try to prove something or exaggerate it. That's when I get mad. Like one time me and my mom were coming from church and we stopped by Grand Ma Biscuits. They backed us in while we were inside. It was a black man and a white woman. And they were standing on his side of the car. I blew the horn for him to move. He wanted to move the car, but she pushed him inside the car and just got all over him and started kissing him and would not move the car.

I was so mad! I was going to get out of the car and go over there and sock her in the mouth. Mama said, Don't go over there. You'll just start some trouble.' I was getting out... Mama begged me and begged me not to get out of the car. And she was looking back. Kissing him and looking back at me to see what I was doing.

I was so mad, I could feel my heart beating. I wanted to get that girl.

[She got out]... and then she walked around the car and got in real slow and sat there and kissed him again. And still would not move the car. Now all I had to do was go in there and call 911.

Finally he got out of the car, closed the door, and walked on. And she drove off.

Was that mean? She did it only because I was black.

And I wanted to get out and whip her tail... My mom was scared... If my mom hadn't had a bad heart, I knew I would have... All day I was so mad. And I knew I should not have paid my mom any mind. It was trash!

He was a nice-looking man. And for him to let her do that, that's what got me. He let her do it. So he was stupid too. So that kind right there, black women don't want anyway.

He should have said, 'No, this is not right.' He shouldn't have let it happen.

[White women] really think that black men like them better than black women.

The white women that I know have said that the guys they were dating had put black women down. They said [black women] were money-hungry or always asking for material things... One woman said that black men say, 'I don't date black women because they always want you to give them something.' And [the white woman] said, 'Well, I wonder what they think we want. We want the same things.'

On dating white men

I felt like I had done something wrong to my black men. I didn't want them to see me. I didn't want them to think I had crossed. It was just a white man that I'd met, who was really nice.

I didn't trust him. I don't trust the white man. I just always thought in the back of my mind that he only wanted me for sex. Or only wanted black women in general for sex...

One time this white man wanted to take me out. He was a doll! He had been begging me for several month and I decided to go out with him, but I had to ask him a question first. So I said, 'Can I ask you something? Would you take me home to your mom and let me meet her?' And he said, 'No.' And I said, 'Why not?' He said, 'She's not that understanding.' And I knew I couldn't date him...

Black Men, Black Women

Black women are not going to obey anybody but themselves. And black men want women to obey them...

Men have told me that I was too outspoken. Or that I was too headstrong. They said I always had to have things go my way. Well, yeah, I had to have things go my way... If I thought their way was right and I thought I could benefit in some way, then I probably would do it. Most of them want us to be tin soldiers and we're not going to be tin soldiers. And I think they get upset with us for being the way we are.

I think a woman has her place in the relationship... to respect him and be there for him. Side by side. Not in the back. Not in the front. Certain times she should speak and certain times she shouldn't speak. Even if her idea is better. Especially in the presence of another man. I don't think you should belittle the man that you are with. But after the people are gone, tell him what you think, then.

I think her place is to be his other half. There are certain parts the woman should play. And there are certain parts the man should play. Some women try to play the man's part, too. Because I've tried it before. I just don't want the man to think he's putting anything over on me.

Black women know what true love is and that's what they try to give... but men always think we are too aggressive.

Black women's definition of love is different from the man's definition of love... Love to black men... I don't even know what they think love is... because when you're giving love, they don't want it. They think you're trying to overpower them... They love, but they try to hide their love. Most men won't say that they love somebody. I think that's because they weren't brought up loving and knowing true love.

I think love is sharing and caring. Love is not apologizing all the time. If they keep doing stuff and they keep saying, 'I'm sorry,' then that's not true love.

Women love differently than men?

Yeah. Women love deep, in a spirit, whereas men [are lustful and more physical]. That's why.... they can be in love with you and then go sleep with another woman. Whereas a woman in general, if she's in love, she cannot sleep with another man. She loves deep. Black women love deep.

Not all men, but most of them... think with their penis.

Do you feel more positive about yourself when you are in a relationship?

I only feel differently when I really really like the guy in my heart... But then after it wears off, I'm back to myself. I don't need a man to feel strong. That's why I don't have one.

Garland, who I'm seeing now, told me the ball is in my court. Now after he gets me, the ball probably won't be in my court. He'll probably call the shots. And that's when I'll get uptight, and I'm not going to let him call the shots because I'm not that way.

Is trust difficult for you?

Yes. Even if he's an angel. I still don't trust him. In the back of mind, I think that something is going to come out.

When people meet each other... they always try to impress and do more in the beginning, when they know they're not that way. But they do that just to get that person. And once they get them, it all stops. And that's when the conflict comes in. Especially the woman, thinking that he's changed. When actually he didn't change...

... People should be real... like me, this is how I am.

Living with the man you're with

It bothered me that my husband [now deceased] didn't compliment me, even though I might get a compliment from somebody else. Why is it someone else can compliment me and he can't? I figured there was something about me he didn't like. I took it personally.

For example, one day my girlfriend Donna and I stopped at the make up counter during our lunch hour... Donna got all made up and she bought all this make-up, [including] false eyelashes. The saleslady put them on me... and they laid back against my eyelids instead of coming out.

We went back to work and had a good time!

My husband picked me up at five. He said, 'Hi.' I said, 'Hi.' We went thorough the motions, 'kiss, kiss.' We went home and I fixed dinner. I sat across from him as he was talking and I began to bat my eyes... He never mentioned it and there was no way in the world, he could miss those eyelashes!

When I mentioned them he said, 'Oh yeah, I noticed. I meant to tell you...'

Stuff like that bothered me. The only reason it didn't bother me more was because I worked outside of the house and I received all these compliments outside. So I knew I must not have been too bad.

He'd tell me what he didn't like. But he never told me what he liked. If I had on something he didn't like, he'd say, 'Oh, where'd you get that dress? I sure don't like that.' If it was a dress he did like, he'd never mention it.

The female ego

There are certain things that every woman knows she's got. It could be pretty legs or pretty hair or figure... You know you've got something. And I think the fact that somebody else recognizes it outside of your house or outside of your relationship is what can carry you along. I think if it was somebody who stayed home all day and they never saw anyone but their husband and their kids, it could be a problem.

But if you get out and go to work and they come out and tell you that you look good... and you know them well enough to know when they're not bluffing and when they are telling the truth, then your ego gets boosted in that way... It isn't like you don't get it at all. If you didn't get it all that would be a problem.

It bothered me when I could see him looking at other women when we went to parties. But I fixed that, my daughter fixed that the time she had me buy a slinky, fringy, white evening dress for a dance. I wore that dress and everybody kept telling me how good I looked. He stayed closer than he usually did. He wasn't all over the place. And then after that, I said to myself, 'I've got to attract other people...'

The Art of Manipulation

Women can manipulate anybody. I used my friend Nadine to re-do my house. At the same time Justin thought it was all his idea.

Everything I asked him to do as far as changing and decorating the house, he wouldn't do. I knew he liked Nadine's house and he valued her opinion. So I told her I decided I wanted to knock out the wall between the living room and the den. Nadine said, 'Oh, you've got to. I can't stand it.' I told her he'd never go for it.

We came up with this idea that she would suggest it. That way, he and I wouldn't get into an argument. Because if I had suggested it, he'd say, 'Oh, you know, you're always trying to get me to spend money.' So one day we're sitting there talking and Nadine said, 'Justin, why don't you do something with this wall? It's ugly. You've got a nice house. Tear that junk out! Spread this house open! Do this! Do that!'

He said, 'I don't want to tear my house down. I didn't buy my house to tear it up.' The same thing he told me. She said, 'Well, you don't want to leave it like this do you?' The next thing I knew his friends were volunteering to help do the work... It wasn't any time before the wall was down.

And so I used that type of psychology to get him to do what I wanted him to do.

Partnerships

You have to find out the best way to be an emotional partner. That depends on the type of man you have in your life. You can't let them think you're feeling sorry for them. Or that you think they aren't doing what you think they're supposed to do. Or that you think they're weak... You have to find your own way of getting to him. It sounds hard but it isn't. And you never let them know what you're doing.

Ella, 70-something

Life and Marriage, Who Ever Said They Would be Easy or Fair?

The whole idea of commitment has changed over the years. What constituted a relationship or marriage is not the same thing that it was years ago. Years ago it didn't have to be spelled out. You thought of it in terms of love. If somebody loved you enough that's what it was [commitment]. Sex, was it satisfying? Or money? There was a standard of money that everyone was expected to have. They certainly weren't expected to be millionaires or billionaires... But accepted for who and what [they] had.

But all of that has changed now. You have lost the three most important things. Which is respect for your spouse. Trust. Understanding. I think those three things are missing in today's relationships. There's nothing to hold onto when times get bad. Everybody's got to split and go their own way.

I think World War II brought about a lot of changes in terms of women working. Your economic situation changed completely... You began to make as much money as the men had made and consequently you didn't want to go back to where you came from...

Men were away in the service, which contributed to a lot of promiscuity that a lot of black women had not

161

participated in wholesale... Over the years white women had been a lot more promiscuous than we had been. But during World War II while the men were gone, some of these black women got ideas of having a good time and so that sort of enhanced the trend. I think the trend was there but I think [the war] sort of enhanced it.

I know it has gotten worse through the years. What has happened is the lack of respect. Men... they don't respect women anymore because women have put themselves out there to be exploited. And they have been exploited to such an extent that the average man never even trusts a woman. You meet someone and unless you know their background and where they came from, where they lived or something about them that somebody can verify, you don't know where they might have been prior to this point.

What were your expectations when you got married?

I guess you take a clue from your family. Your mother and father, and what you'd been exposed to in your own household. At that time young ladies kept their dress down. You didn't have a lot of sex without being ostracized... You didn't have babies... If there was a child, there would be a mother and father there for that child. Even though times might get tough, you stuck it out. You stayed there at least until the child was old enough to take care of itself.

I think we women had a tendency to try to cover for the men back then. You didn't let people on the outside know what was going on inside your house. Because men have always run around. They've always done that and I believe they're going to always do that. But I don't think it was quite as wholesale as it is now. I think they thought a little bit more of it than they have in recent years.

Marriage was supposed to be like you had read about, I guess. You go to work and you come home and prepare home. You both work towards the child. Be with and support the child in its little activities... no big thing.

Today... expectations are just not the same as they were years ago. The man isn't expected to be loyal to one woman anymore... He can fall into the gutter, pick himself up and brush himself off and keep on going... I think

162

he has a little bit more responsibility towards the whole thing than he is being asked to assume.

The Realities of a Marriage

Before you get married, I really advocate and I mean this, you really need to sit down and talk. Talk about everything. To find out where these people are coming from. Because you don't know some of these people. I'll say, 'Why didn't you tell me this?' And he'll say, 'You never asked.'

Money is a problem in marriage. I ain't going to tell no lie about that. That is one of the basic things...When most couples break up, somewhere back there money is involved. Somebody didn't pay some bills. Or somebody expects too much. Or somebody feels the other person is spending too much money.

The basic problem with my husband and I has been that we are not really compatible. Our likes and dislikes... I didn't realize this until I had been in the marriage for some years.

Sometimes this love stuff overpowers the real basic things that you need. You see, because love is going to vanish. It's going out the window after a period of time. The sex part is going out the window after a period of time and you need something there that you can hold on to. What do you have left in the marriage when you remove those two things? What is left are the important things. Because if you live long enough those things are going to disappear. They just don't stay the same. You don't feel the same way.

In my husband's case, he's a lot like my daughter. They both want to start at the top. They don't want to take the little jobs and work up. That want to start up here, in charge. And it doesn't work that way. I'm willing to work my way up. I'm willing to give the time, the effort, the energy, whatever is necessary, because I know where I want to go and I'm willing to pay the price to get there. I also know that in this life, you've got to have enough money to pay bills. You've got to pay those bills. Somebody's got to pay them... take your money and pay them.

We put our money together when we first got married and it didn't work out. I spent very little of the money because I'd say, 'I know what we've got to do.' When it came time to pay, the pot was a little empty. 'Hey, where'd it go?' I said. 'It didn't just get up and walk away. Somebody took it.' He said, 'Well, I needed this and I needed that.' And so I don't know until the end. And I'm ticked! 'This was not your money! It was our money! I put money in here too!'

There are couples who are still doing it that way now. But it didn't take me long to see it wouldn't work for us... You should write on a piece of paper, 'You pay this. I pay that.' And when the time comes and you don't have your part of the money, that's your problem, it ain't mine. I found out I had to do that in order to keep my head above water. Some people are just better at handling money than others. Some people are just stronger than other people.

I worked and took a whole lot of stuff on my job. I wanted to kick two or three people over the years when I was working, but I didn't dare do that. I had a job. Bills had to be paid. Things had to keep going, so I stayed on the job and took it whatever it was.

You kind of look to your man for strength, for somebody to lean on. Not for the man to lean on you. Because even though we as black women are strong women, you get tired. You get tired of that, you know. You'd like for somebody to share this burden, because it gets mighty heavy sometimes. And you want somebody who's going to say, 'Don't worry about it. It's going to be all right.' That's all you want to hear. It may not be true, but you'd like to hear it. 'It's going to be all right.'

And I find too... they say all women are supposed to come home and say, 'Honey, how was your day? Did you have a nice day?' Get his slippers and run his bath and all of that. I want to see where it says that he's supposed to do that for me. I'm sharing that responsibility just like he is and perhaps a lot more. Because then after I leave my job, I've got to come home and I've got another job waiting for me then. And I kind of resent that. I really do. I kind of resent that I've got to be so strong...

... I like a strong man. I like a man with strength that I can see and feel. Not by beating up a woman or anything like that. But one who knows where he wants to go and knows how to get there and is willing to go along with the program.

After a while the reason why we stay together so long is, it has been 47 years. It's not because it has been 47 years of a real wonderful time. But you stay because of your child. Because after a certain point in your life I don't think it really makes much difference.

A war of the sexes?

I see black men with white women a little more now. [Years ago] you had to go to certain sections of the country. When I see them, I say, 'That black man sure in heaven now... that's as close as he's ever going to get.'

I think it gives him freedom. That's the funny thing about life, everything you want to do that they say is bad for you always seems to be the most thrilling or exciting things to do.

White women are submissive to their men. Whereas black women don't take no stuff. And black men don't like that. They like being in charge. I tell you it's a power thing. It's not just a black thing, it's a power thing. Can I control you. If he tells the white woman, 'Bring home your money and give it to me,' she'll do that. A black woman will say, 'You must be kidding."

17

Kaleiding With Destiny

One of the most difficult aspects for me to grasp of the plight of black men and women and the African-American community at large has been accepting that there are people who are not products of misfortune, but who choose to live their lives with complete disregard for their own well-being, as well as others', all the while equipped with the values and awareness to live a healthy, productive life. In other words, some just don't give a damn. These people by choice shirk the values or responsibilities they were raised under in various ways. Maybe by raising their children with a loose hand or not at all. Maybe by turning to drugs or alcohol. Maybe with dishonesty and lack of commitment in their relationships. When played out, these type of actions snowball and have an impact on how all interested parties relate to themselves and other people.

One night riding home on the subway, I noticed a man and woman across from me. Beside the woman was a young boy eight or nine years old, who appeared to be their son. On the floor between the man's legs, in a portable carrier, was a newborn baby, asleep, seemingly only days old. I had difficulty containing my emotions at the sight of this beautiful child on the floor. There was plenty of room to place the carrier beside the father on a seat.

When I managed to overcome my fear of the baby hitting his head against the bottom of the seat as the carrier rocked, or someone swiping his head with their bag as they passed by, I glanced at the parents and tried to figure out what type of people they were that they thought it was okay to place a baby on the dirty floor of a subway car.

The father had a kind face, but still, the child was on the floor. At times he didn't even hold onto the handle of the carrier, despite the fact the train was going at a high rate of speed. The mother never appeared to look at the child. She just seemed happy to be the object of her man's affection as he held and caressed her.

Then I looked at the older son. Outwardly he seemed well-adjusted. But I had to wonder what he was learning from these two people. What did it mean to him to see this fragile, delicate child placed on the floor exposed to imminent danger? Did it suggest to him (as it did to me) that the child was of little importance? Was it inevitable, subconsciously at least, that over a period of time he would likewise feel unimportant or of little value after observing his parents' casual regard for an innocent infant? And lastly, with his parents as role models, I wondered how the boy would treat the child.

Every adult generation has their mind's eye vision of what has been lost on the youth of present day. What I recognize is my fear of the disappearance of the African-American family. What I see is a disparity between healthy, financially sound households and those that are less affluent. These households cannot relate to each other. They are at opposite extremes. And across the board are individuals whose actions reflect indifference to the problems that plague the future of African-American communities.

We commonly fault the white man for our plight. The black community may be inevitably linked to the white community, but the white community does not control the black community's destiny and survival. That responsibility rests within us. It is a responsibility that many of our parents shared from household to household, family to family, as they led us into adulthood. Then something changed. Something stopped. And it cannot be blamed on the white man. Because in spite of him, many parents laid foundations and provided opportunities to enable their children to build healthy, successful lives. And now with our education (be it from the streets or institutions) and success, many experience difficulty creating and maintaining lasting relationships. Women are pessimistic about their chances of marrying a black male. Black men are exploring options beyond black women. And we have a new generation of children, half of whom we want to "write off" off as a bad debt and the other half of whom we criticize for what appears to be a lack of interest and respect for their history and the road that was paved for them. Collectively, our achievement and success has not been utilized in a positive way.

We are all different. We don't all care to the same degree. If people want to see improvements and change come about in relationships and in their communities, seemingly simple, but actually difficult tasks are in order. An actual movement is in order toward repairing and improving our relationships because although the state that we are in took years to create, we do not have an unlimited amount of time to alter it. Because soon the children of our generation, some whom have their own children, will be unreceptive, consciously or unconsciously, to any positive messages we attempt to send their way.

There must be a starting point with any movement or change. In this case it must begin within ourselves. There must be a desire to recognize the aspects of our lives that limit us and destroy our relationships. Leo was on point earlier when he suggested that his wife felt that if he did not shortchange himself, he would not shortchange her. Remember that old saying, 'If you look good, you feel good. If you feel good, you do good'? It is the same premise. Most people by nature have a preoccupation with their own needs. In the same vein, if a person can recognize what compromises their inner spirit and value system, they will be a mentally and emotionally healthier person and partner. The practice of acknowledging what makes you unhappy, happy, creates an inner awareness and honesty that can enable you to be true to yourself and avoid potentially damaging situations.

True self-awareness is a difficult accomplishment, but it is not enough. Those of us who care must be better people. If it is true that we are lying, we must be more honest. If it is true that we are being irresponsible, we must be more considerate and respectful. If it is true we are generating myths, we must be less self-centered. The future of the African-American community depends on it. Not the future of America or American society. Not the future of the world. But the future of the African-American community depends on how black men and women continue to treat each other and raise their children.

The time for personal responsibility is here. With regard to my personal relationships, it has not been easy for me to examine. I have had to realize that I am an important component in my relationships and along with my role is my share of responsibility. I let go of myself by not being true to my needs. In most cases when conflicts arose, I let them go unaddressed or I tolerated them in the end, in an effort to keep the man in my life. In doing so, I diminished my value in the relationship. Josh and Sonny were not at fault for this. When it became obvious that I was not going to receive what I was giving, I should have trusted my instincts and left for greener pastures. But I didn't. Instead I continued on against my better judgment and interests and little by little relinquished my personal responsibility and power.

Is there any common thread beyond the frustrations and differences men and women expressed? Everyone has needs they would like to see addressed. Throughout the interviewing process I noticed that many men have needs that women are not aware of. And women have needs that men do not wish to address. Again it comes down to a desire to educate yourself to your mate's needs without reservations.

Women should love their men enough to be sensitive to his experiences in the world and attentive to his desires. There is something wrong if, for example, I don't realize that my man enjoys himself most when the two of us are alone and I always invite a group of friends. There is something wrong if I don't realize what makes my man tick, what sets him off, what makes him laugh, or what hurts him.

Men should be tuned in to these sensitivities in women as well. I believe in many cases they have a clearer insight. However, they oftentimes deny women their experiences of frustration, anger, or disappointment by attempting to suppress these emotions in women when they threaten to surface. If a woman is disappointed with her man, she should have the freedom to express that disappointment without his resentment over her emotions. She is capable of understanding his reasons and at the same time feeling disappointment. For example, I can discover the reasons for my man's actions, which displeased me, understand and still be angry. I may have to get over it to move forward. But I should not be denied the experience of my fury.

The act of disregarding our mates' needs or denying the experience of emotions can create an atmosphere of inhibitions, disrespect, and negativity. These are aspects of our relationships that we must examine. We must identify and communicate our own needs and those of our mate. We must understand that together they must be nurtured and the nurturing is an ongoing process.